TWAYNE'S WORLD AUTHORS SERIES
A Survey of the World's Literature

GERMANY

Ulrich Weisstein, Indiana University

EDITOR

Friedrich Schiller

TWAS 603

Friedrich Schiller

Portrait by C. von Kügelen, engraved by Posselwhite

FRIEDRICH SCHILLER

By JOHN D. SIMONS

Florida State University

TWAYNE PUBLISHERS

A DIVISION OF G. K. HALL & CO., BOSTON

Library of Congress Cataloging in Publication Data

Simons, John D.
Friedrich Schiller.

(Twayne's world authors series ; TWAS 603. Germany)
Bibliography: p. 155
Includes index.
1. Schiller, Friedrich, 1759-1805—Criticism and interpretation.
I. Series.
PT2492.S54   831'.6   81-4908
ISBN 0-8057-6445-3   AACR2

To Ursula
Mary
Lois
Steve

Contents

About the Author

John D. Simons was born and raised near Dallas, Texas. After graduating from high school, his father sent him to study at the university in Göttingen, Germany. Returning to the United States in 1957, he attended the University of Texas. After completing the course work for the M.A. he wrote the thesis at the Bibliothèque Nationale, Paris. This was followed by another year in Munich. In 1966 he received the Ph.D. from Rice, writing on *Schiller's Influence on Dostoevsky*. He is the author of several scholarly articles and monographs on various figures in German and Russian literature. He travels widely in Europe and North and South America. In 1977 he joined an oceanographic expedition to Antarctica as participating humanist. He now teaches at The Florida State University.

Preface

Another book on Schiller? Why, according to his bibliographers, nearly three dozen have appeared since 1900 alone—which works out roughly to a book every two years. When we take into account the vast number of essays and monographs, he ranks as one of the world's most explicated authors. Why add another? The present addition will seem more justified if we consider that only three of those books hail from this country. All the rest document what Schiller means to Europeans and to their time. This volume fills the need for a study telling what he means to us today in the United States.

The book is oriented toward the nonspecialist. Concentrating on the fundamentals, it covers aesthetics, poetry, and drama which are the three main "genre" in which Schiller was active. Since the poetry and the drama are more meaningful when read in the light of his ideas about art, politics, and the human condition, I discuss the theoretical writings first. Chapter 1 is therefore the foundation on which the following three rest. Occasionally I use examples from other well-known authors to illustrate some of his ideas. At the same time, these examples are more than an aid to comprehension because they also serve to illustrate Schiller's universality.

Chapter 2 concentrates on the poetry, chapters 3 and 4 on the dramas. The exposition of each work under consideration follows a form specified by the publisher of the series. A brief account of the genesis of the piece is followed by a summary of the elements of the plot. A critical analysis of the work rounds out the survey. The conclusion presents Schiller's ideas which have exerted the greatest influence on the development of thought in the fields of aesthetics, political theory, and psychology.

The treatment of so prolific a writer as Schiller requires selection. I have omitted his historical writings because they have less to say to our time than to his. I have left out *The Ghostseer* and *Demetrius* because they are fragments. I have excluded *On Grace and Dignity*, *Kallias Letters*, and other theoretical writings to concentrate in depth upon his major essays *On the Aesthetic Education of Man* and *On Naive and Sentimental Poetry.* I have not discussed Schiller's relationship to Aristotle, Plato, Kant, Goethe, and other thinkers and writers to avoid overburdening the text. I have refrained from taking issue with the views of my colleagues for the same reason.

Wherever possible I use translations that are now in print or easily available in the library. For the essay on aesthetics I use Wilkinson and Willoughby's dual language edition *On the Aesthetic Education of Man;* for the essay on poetry, Julius A. Elias's *Naive and Sentimental Poetry,* which is available in paperback; for the drama, Charles E. Passage. My colleague Miroslav John Hanak translated the poetry. English renditions from *The Robbers* and all other works are my own.

I want to thank my colleagues Hans Braendlin, Leon Golden, and Helga Kraft for valuable suggestions; and especially Ursula, who worked with me from the beginning, listening, discussing, reading, revising.

JOHN D. SIMONS

The Florida State University

Chronology

1759 Born 10 November, Johann Christoph Friedrich Schiller, at Marbach on the Neckar. Son of Johann Caspar Schiller and Elizabeth. The father was an officer in the army of the renowned despot Karl Eugen, duke of Württemberg.

1773 The duke orders young Schiller to enroll in his new military academy, the *Karlsschule*, where he studies first law, then medicine.

1776 Instruction in philosophy by Professor Abel.

1779 Submits dissertation *Die Philosophie der Physiologie* [The Philosophy of Physiology]. The committee rejects it.

1780 Completes first draft of *Die Räuber* [The Robbers]. Submits a new dissertation *Über den Zusammenhang der tierischen Natur des Menschen mit seiner geistigen* [On the Relationship between Man's Animal and Spiritual Nature]. Committee accepts the dissertation. Begins to serve as regimental surgeon after graduation in December.

1781 Publishes his drama *Die Räuber* at his own expense.

1782 13 January, director of the Mannheim Theater, Dalberg, stages first performance of *Die Räuber*. It is a phenomenal success. Publishes collection of poetry *Anthologie auf das Jahr 1782* [Anthology for the Year 1782]. August, the duke forbids Schiller to write anything except essays on medicine. September, Schiller deserts the army and flees to Mannheim. Dalberg refuses to help. Fearing reprisals from the duke, Schiller goes underground. Hides out near the village Bauerbach where he completes his next play *Die Verschwörung des Fiesko zu Genua* [The Fiesko Conspiracy at Genoa].

1783 Completes another drama, *Kabale und Liebe* [Love and Intrigue]. Begins work on his fourth play, *Don Carlos*. July, moves to Mannheim, where he has a one-year contract to write dramas for Dalberg.

1784 11 January, first performance of *Fiesko*. 15 April, first performance of *Kabale und Liebe*. Reads the first act of

Don Carlos to the visiting Duke Karl August von Sachsen-Weimar. The duke awards him the title of *Hofrat*.

1785 First issue of the literary journal *Rheinische Thalia*, which Schiller founds. April, moves to Leipzig as Gottfried Körner's guest. Writes poetry. Moves to Dresden. The short story *Der Verbrecher aus Verlorener Ehre* [The Criminal from Lost Honor].

1787 June, completes *Don Carlos*. Completes the major historical tract *Abfall der vereinigten Niederlande* [Revolt of the United Netherlands]. Visits Weimar where he meets Wieland and other literary figures.

1788 The poem "Die Götter Griechenlands" [The Gods of Greece]. "Briefe über Don Carlos" [Letters on Don Carlos]. Goethe keeps his distance from Schiller, but recommends him for the vacancy in the History Department at the University of Jena.

1789 Accepts the offer to teach history at the University of Jena. Poem "Die Künstler" [The Artists]. The essay *Die Gesetzgebung des Lykurgos und Solon* [The Laws of Lycurgos and Solon]. The fragment *Der Geisterseher* [The Ghostseer].

1790 Receives a guaranteed salary. Marries Charlotte von Lengefeld. *Über die tragische Kunst* [On Tragic Art]. *Geschichte des dreissigjährigen Kriegs* [History of the Thirty Years War].

1791 Falls seriously ill and nearly dies. He suffers from this disease, probably tuberculosis, for the rest of his life. December, receives a three-year pension from the Danish court.

1792 Studies Kant.

1793 Exchanges letters with Körner on the concept of beauty, *Die Kallias-Briefe* [The Kallias Letters]; *Über Anmut und Würde* [On Grace and Dignity]; *Über das Erhabene* [On the Sublime]. His desertion now forgotten, Schiller visits Stuttgart and the *Karlsschule*.

1794 He works on the drama *Wallenstein* and on the essay *Über die ästhetische Erziehung des Menschen* [On the Aesthetic Education of Man], which he completes the next summer. Beginning of the friendship with Goethe.

1795 "Der Tanz" [The Dance]; "Das Ideal und das Leben" [The Ideal and Life]; "Das verschleierte Bild zu Sais" [The

Veiled Image at Sais]; "Der Spaziergang" [The Walk]; "Pegasus im Joch" [Pegasus Yoked]; *Musenalmanach für das Jahr 1796.* Works on the essay *Über naive und sentimentalische Dichtung* [On Naive and Sentimental Poetry].

1796   Schelling and Jean Paul visit Schiller in Jena. Schiller and Goethe collaborate on *Xenien.*

1797   "Der Taucher" [The Diver]; "Der Handschuh" [The Glove]; "Der Ring des Polykrates" [The Ring of Polykrates]; "Die Kraniche des Ibykus" [The Cranes of Ibykus]; "Der Gang nach dem Eisenhammer" [The Trip to the Forge]. Buys some property in Jena for a retreat.

1798   Poetry: "Der Kampf mit dem Drachen" [The Fight with the Dragon]; "Die Bürgschaft" [The Hostage]; "Das Eleusische Fest" [The Eleusinian Festival]. 12 October *Wallensteins Lager* [Wallenstein's Camp] premieres. Hard work on *Die Piccolomini.*

1799   Completes *Wallenstein.* Goethe stages the trilogy in its entirety. Completes the first three acts of *Maria Stuart.* Moves to Weimar across the street from Goethe. Close association with the *Weimar Hoftheater.* Poetry: "Das Lied von der Glocke" [The Song of the Bell], which appears in his *Musenalmanach auf das Jahr 1800.*

1800   The *Wallenstein* trilogy appears in book form. *Maria Stuart* premieres 14 June.

1801   11 September, the premiere of *Die Jungfrau von Orleans* [The Maiden of Orleans]. Poetry: "Sehnsucht" [Longing].

1802   Receives patent of nobility in recognition of his literary accomplishments. Poetry: "An die Freunde" [To Friends]; "Die Vier Weltalter" [The Four Ages of the World]; "Kassandra".

1803   19 March, premiere of *Die Braut von Messina* [The Bride of Messina]. Poetry: "Das Siegesfest" [The Victory Feast].

1804   17 March, first performance of *Wilhelm Tell,* an enormous success. 26 April, travels to Berlin to attend a festival in his honor. Duke Karl August doubles Schiller's salary to keep him in Weimar. Schiller stays in Weimar working on his next drama *Demetrius,* which remains a fragment.

1805   Schiller falls mortally ill. He dies on 9 May.

CHAPTER 1

Aesthetics

I *On the Aesthetic Education of Man in a Series of Letters*

SCHILLER'S most important contribution to aesthetics owes its existence, at least in part to the generosity of one of his admirers, Prince Friedrich Christian, duke of Schleswig-Holstein-Augustenburg. Learning in 1791 that Schiller was convalescing from a bout with tuberculosis, the prince granted him a stipend of one thousand thalers per annum for three consecutive years. Freed from financial worries, Schiller soon recovered sufficiently to continue his study of history and philosophy. His essay in letter form *On the Aesthetic Education of Man* is the direct result of this period of intense intellectual activity. The work developed out of a correspondence with the prince, in the course of which Schiller revealed his thoughts on the relationship of art and beauty to life, to politics, and to social evolution. Published in 1795, this work, along with *On Naive and Sentimental Poetry*, forms the core of his aesthetic.[1]

The *Aesthetic Letters* represent Schiller's view of man and of the civilizations which he creates. Underlying the essay is Schiller's belief that man and his institutions gradually evolve toward a higher moral plane. Since the historical events of the eighteenth century— especially in France—hardly supported his theory, Schiller had to come to terms with these contemporary realities, propose a remedy, and prescribe ways of improving the human condition.

Schiller's approach in this essay can be likened to a medical examination, a procedure with which he was familiar from both the doctor's and the patient's point of view. A physician comes to a medical examination with a thorough understanding of both human anatomy and body chemistry. He begins the examination by identifying the symptoms of the patient. Then he diagnoses the malady and its underlying cause. Finally he prescribes a cure. He explains how the prescription works and tells the patient how to stay healthy.

Applying this metaphor to Schiller's essay, his theory can be epitomized in a few statements which serve as introduction to the exposition that follows.

The physician is Schiller, the patient man and society, and the ailment stagnation. The lower classes display the symptoms of violence, selfishness, and superstition. Perversity, decay, egotism, and moral shallowness pervade the cultivated class. The underlying cause is found in the imbalance between man's animal and rational drives, a condition that certain developments in civilization itself exacerbate—such as overspecialization. The two drives must be made to work in unison before mankind can resume its upward course (letters 1–9). Schiller prescribes beauty as the proper medicine. Beauty has remarkable healing powers because it works on both drives at once to bring them into better balance (letters 10–18). Since Schiller believes that the social system reflects the character of its citizens, man improves society by improving himself. Improvement comes about through aesthetic education; that is, by cultivating the faculty for appreciating beauty (letters 19–27). The following pages are an exposition of this theory, which is structured according to Schiller's own pattern. There are three main sections. The first introduces his theory of social evolution, and his views on man and society and what ails them. The second concerns play, beauty, and art, which the author prescribes as a cure to the malady exposed in the first section. The third treats artistic semblance and the aesthetic state with the object of showing their relation to everyday living and to social evolution.

A   *The Natural State and the Moral State*

Schiller devotes much of the first section to developing the thesis that man as individual and civilization as a whole progress through definite stages. Both begin in the natural state, *Naturstaat*, and both develop toward the moral state, *Moralstaat*. The natural state is that of man in earliest epochs before he perfects his faculty of reason. In this condition he is a creature determined and protected by nature. Like the lower animals, he lives in a kind of involuntary servitude compelled by instinct, driven by appetites, and tortured by physical needs. His value system is strictly utilitarian: Whatever promotes survival is good and whatever threatens it bad. Nothing else exists for him. Eventually, the need for protection drives him to organize into haphazard social units and the natural state arises, which is "jeder politischer Körper der seine Einrichtung ursprünglich von

Kräften, nicht von Gesetzen ableitet." ("any political body whose organization derives originally from forces and not from laws," III, 3).[2] Since natural man cannot be relied upon to obey the law of his own free will, the primitive political body maintains order by brute force.

Fortunately, man is not locked into this state, as are the lower animals. For he has a rational faculty which, when once awakened, tears him away from nature and empowers him to transform compulsion into free choice. "Jeder Mensch," he says in the *Fourth Letter*, "trägt der Anlage und Bestimmung nach, einen reinen idealischen Menschen in sich" ("Every individual human being carries within him, potentially and perceptively, an ideal man, the archetype of a human being," IV, 2). And he says that not only does every man have the potential to approximate this image but it is also his life's task.

Unlike the natural state, which is based on need, the moral state arises from reason and is based on principles. Moral man differs from natural man in that his rational faculty is developed to the point where it equals his appetites in strength. In this condition each drive has sufficient power to keep the other within its own territory, so that neither interferes with the operation of the other. Consequently, neither sense nor reason compel moral man, but rather both at once. "Beide Gesetzgebungen sollen vollkommen unabhängig von einander bestehen, und dennoch vollkommen einig sein" ("Both these systems of rule are meant to co-exist, in perfect independence of each other, and yet in perfect accord" XXIV, 8). Up to this point, Schiller has been speaking theoretically. Actually, he says, there is no evidence that human beings ever existed as merely sensual or as purely moral beings.

Contemporary society, Schiller says at the beginning of the *Fifth Letter*, does not resemble at all the ideal he envisions. The eighteenth century confronts the spectacle of the natural state hovering on the brink of collapse, awakening hopes—especially in France— for social improvement. Unfortunately, any effort to better the political organization will fail if we do not improve the multitude first. The untrained citizen cannot cope with highly advanced moral principles that demand—among other things—discipline, will-power, respect for human dignity, and detachment from material things. It is impossible to remedy the citizen's deficiencies overnight. Social unrest follows any attempt to do so. Schiller points to the French Revolution to confirm the validity of this fact: as soon as the

old order disintegrated, the citizens pinpointed their low position on
the ladder of evolution. Like madmen, the French fell with unrestrained ferocity upon one another and upon their oppressors. These
events prove to Schiller that the average man was unable to handle
his new rights. When the doors of opportunity swung open, he was
unable to walk through. The reformers in Paris made the mistake of
changing the government not knowing that the prerequisite of a
successful new social order is a citizenry prepared for it.

Moreover, the course of events in revolutionary France proved to
Schiller that the members of the cultivated class were as ill-prepared
to cope with political reform as were their social inferiors. Despite
courtly refinement and intellectual pretensions their interests cen-
tered in the natural state. They led wasteful, self-indulgent, mean-
ingless lives. All the glorious achievements of the Enlightenment
had little, if any, affect in redeeming their spiritual poverty. From
all over Europe the odor of moral decay emanated from this class.
Even those seemingly well prepared turned into intellectual animals
who quickly subverted the principles of the new rationalism into
justifying their depravity. Unguided by moral belief, the impulse to
self-improvement stifled by the fear of losing its power and privilege,
the cultivated class drowned in a cesspool of decadence. Thus the
spirit of Schiller's age manifested itself in the two extremes of
savagery and lethargy, "die zwei Äussersten des menschlichen
Verfalls, und beide in *einem* Zeitraum vereinigt!" ("the two extremes of human depravity, and both united in a *single* epoch," V,
3). What caused this social calamity?

In the *Sixth Letter* Schiller puts most of the blame for man's ills
on overspecialization. First, technological advances created the need
of particular skills. Accordingly, society began to fragment into a
multitude of autonomous compartments inhabited by specialists. As
a consequence, the state separated from the church, laws from
customs, enjoyment from labor, means from ends, effort from
reward. Can it therefore be any wonder that "the inner unity of
human nature was severed too, and a disastrous conflict set its
harmonious powers at variance?" (VI, 6) Thus Schiller diagnoses
the malady of his age as psychic imbalance caused by overspecialization.

By "specialization" Schiller means channeling all the energy into
mastering a particular subject within a profession or business, or
adapting a single skill or talent to one particular function. This is an
affliction all too familiar to us in the twentieth century. It is as

unnatural as it is undesirable. Because, although specialization leads civilization as a whole to fulfillment, it dehumanizes its citizens. In a specialized society, the individual becomes a tool subordinate to the whole, valued according to his usefulness. Schiller praises man's faculty for specialization. He deplores its abuses. Human beings possess numerous faculties, all of which he must exercise in the interests of a harmoniously balanced character. Here Schiller digresses to make some unfavorable comparisons between his own age and that of the ancient Greeks, who knew the value of balance.

In ancient Athens, for instance, the well-rounded individual was expected to be able to play a musical instrument, compose an ode, deliver an oration, serve as a statesman, manage his estate, defend his country, compete in sports, and so on. This ancient ideal has been replaced by the man who knows everything about something and nothing about anything else. There are doctors, lawyers, professors, etc., but few human beings. For the sake of civilization, Schiller says, we must promote inner harmony. Yet we cannot look to the present political organization for help in this enterprise because it is both the cause and the propagator of the malady. Neither can we look to reason, he says in the *Eighth Letter*, because although its task is to conceive and to establish law, it has no power to enforce it. Instead, we must take our cue from the way nature works. As nature evolved all the lower life forms before turning to the highest, so we should begin by refining the animal in man before we try to make him moral.

After establishing that we can rely neither on the state nor on reason to facilitate the improvement of man, Schiller finally prescribes the right medicine in the *Ninth Letter:* "Dieses Werkzeug ist die schöne Kunst." ("This instrument is Fine Art," IX, 2). How does the process work? It involves man's mimetic faculty. Not only do men imitate one another in learning how to speak and in how to express their feelings, they imitate even more what they see on the stage, a canvas, the printed page, or in recent times, television. Art, good or bad, shapes man's value system. Values exist because we perceive them; and what we perceive, and how we perceive them depends on the arts. We prize authenticity, individuality, and freedom because creative individuals have instructed us in their value. Friedrich Nietzsche also comments on this subject in *Götzendämmerung* [The Twilight of the Idols]: "Was tut alle Kunst? lobt sie nicht? verherrlicht sie nicht? wählt sie nicht aus? zieht sie nicht hervor? Mit dem allem *stärkt* oder *schwächt* sie gewisse

Wertschätzungen" ("What does all art do? Does it not praise? Does it not glorify? Does it not select? Does it not bring things into prominence? In all this it *strengthens* and *weakens* certain valuations").[3] The first principle of Schiller's, and later Nietzsche's, theory of art therefore is, *art is the expression of values.* The second principle is, *life imitates art,* not the other way around: "So schreitet sie [der Natur] auch in der Begeisterung, bildend und erweckend, voran." ("Thus art. goes before [Nature], a voice rousing from slumber and preparing the shape of things to come"). Not only does man learn by imitating, he transforms himself into what he imitates. To improve the citizen, "verjage die Willkür, die Frivolität, die Rohigkeit aus ihren Vergnügungen, so wirst du sie unvermerkt auch aus ihren Handlungen, endlich aus ihren Gesinnungen verbannen" ("Banish from their pleasures caprice, frivolity, and coarseness, and imperceptibly you will banish these from their actions and, eventually, from their inclinations too," IX, 7).

Now if man imitates art, the artists of the world are mankind's true shapers. This is an awesome responsibility, and Schiller has some advice to give. The artist must not cater to public wants. His task is not to entertain but to elevate man, to free him from his animal nature. He must give the citizen art to imitate that will ennoble his character: "leiste deinen Zeitgenossen, aber was sie bedürfen, nicht was sie loben" ("work for your contemporaries; but create what they need, not what they praise," IX, 7). Art functions as the instrument of progress because it shapes character. Thus, according to Schiller's theory of social evolution, by means of art man ascends from the natural state to the moral state. Exactly how this process works is the subject of the following section.

B   *Play and Beauty*

In letters 10 to 18 Schiller identifies the conflicting and deterministic forces operating within and on the psyche, with the object of showing how they can be neutralized through play and beauty. He begins by establishing that the psyche is subject to compulsion from two sources. The impulses arising from the animal nature he calls the sense-drive, *Stofftrieb.* The one arising from the rational faculty, he calls the form-drive, *Formtrieb.* I will now discuss these drives in more detail.

The sense-drive includes sense perception, the emotions, and such basics as feeding, fleeing, fighting, and procreation. In short, the sense-drive designates those things which we share with the other animals. This side of our psyche is passive in nature; that is, it requires outside stimulation to be brought into action. The sense of taste, for instance, is aroused only when something is placed on the tongue. Emotions are brought into play by wants. For Schiller, an inactive sense or emotion has no actuality, only a potential. Consequently, the sense-drive demands constant activity. It thrives on experience, manifold stimulation, flux. The object of this drive, in short is "life," *Leben* (XV, 2). It has no goal beyond immediate experience. Because this drive relies on outside stimulation, it is grounded in something beyond our control which Schiller identifies as time, chance, and changing circumstance. It follows that the purely sensate man has no power to determine the course of his life. Instead, he is the object of capricious forces which sweep him back and forth like sand along the beach. When this drive functions exclusively, we have the highest degree of limitation.

The form-drive, on the other hand, designates the operations of the rational faculty. It is the originator of those things which have existence only in the human mind and which could not exist without it: the laws of science, for example, and such abstractions as truth, justice, right, and duty. This side of our psyche is inherently active; that is, it is constantly ordering and creating. It devises standards for judgment and methods of procedure. It creates laws and principles which it applies to everything we experience and feel and organizes it into a unity that has meaning for us. In so doing, it preserves our identity through the changing conditions of the world around us. When we act according to principles, as for example when we practice justice for its own sake, we transcend time and have treated one moment of our life as if it were eternity (XIII, 5). In short, the object of the form-drive is "form."

Thus it would appear that man is composed of two irreconcilable drives which pull him in opposite directions. One demands change, the other permanence. One says: act on inclination, the other: act on principle. One thrives on sense experience, the other on autonomous activity.

Schiller claims that the drives are not contradictory by nature, "und wenn sie demohngeachtet so erscheinen, so sind sie es erst geworden durch eine freie Übertretung der Natur, indem sie sich selbst missverstehen und ihre Sphären verwirren" ("and if they nevertheless seem to be so, it is because they have become opposed through a wanton transgression of nature, through mistaking their nature and function, and confusing their spheres of operation,"

XIII, 2). Appearances to the contrary, the drives conflict only in their tendencies, not in their objects. The object of the sense-drive is "life." It demands change, but only in experience—not in principles or in laws. The object of the form-drive is "form." It demands permanence, but only in laws—not in sensation or in experience. Thus things that do not meet cannot come into conflict. Trouble arises only when one of them is developed to the exclusion of the other. Both drives have to interact in harmony for any meaningful activity to occur.

Schiller observes that, more often than not, the drives are out of balance within most of us, as we experience one of them exclusively or both alternately. Rarely do we have an intellectual and an emotional experience at the same time. But suppose on occasion we thought and felt at once and in harmony? Whenever opposites interact in concert, they synthesize into a third, which Schiller identifies as "play" (Spiel). Play itself transcends this equilibrium by merging the two drives into a higher synthesis. There is a good metaphorical example of play as synthesis in the ballad Das Lied von der Glocke: as tin and copper combine to produce bronze, so the sense-drive and the form-drive fuse to produce play.

"Play" is the most important concept in the essay. It refers to activity for its own sake. It is something done as an end in itself without any secondary motive of profit. We play games, sing, dance, take a walk, or paint a picture purely for the pleasure involved. Our delight in play appears to derive precisely from its nonutilitarian character. If it could be turned to some account, our delight in it would cease because our attention would be transferred to whatever we could get with it, and play would become work. Seen in this way, play and work take on a different meaning and are equivalent to freedom and servitude. By work Schiller means what is done from necessity or for reward, by play whatever is done for its own sake.

The play state of being constitutes wholeness, totality, simultaneity; it signifies the union of such opposites as permanence and transitoriness, order and chaos, duty and inclination. The play-drive (Spieltrieb) can be thought of as the force that permeates the psyche and binds it together. This side of our psyche is both active and passive at once, it produces and receives at the same time. Play works its magic by satisfying simultaneously both the demands of the flesh and those of the spirit. For man, it is only play "was ihn vollständig macht und seine doppelte Natur auf einmal entfaltet" ("makes man whole and unfolds both sides of his nature at once,"

XV, 7). And the famous words: "der Mensch spielt nur, wo er in voller Bedeutung des Worts Mensch ist, und *er ist nur da ganz Mensch, wo er spielt*" ("man only plays when he is in the fullest sense of the word a human being, and he is only a human being when he plays," XV, 9). If we can imagine a purely playful man, it is one who transcends mind and body, and is truly free.

Schiller's theory culminates in the *Fifteenth Letter* when he says that play and beauty are compounded of the same elements: If the object of the sense-drive is life, and that of the form-drive form, then the object of the play-drive is "living form" (*lebende Gestalt*); that is, "was man in weitester Bedeutung *Schönheit* nennt" ("what in the widest sense of the term we call *beauty*," XV, 2). Like play, beauty is compounded of two elements. It is form because we think it, and life because we feel it. Like play, it is a state of our being and an activity we perform. Like play, its value is intrinsic. Like play, it gives us something to enjoy passively and to imitate actively. Now if play and beauty are alike, that means that both have the same synthesizing effect on the psyche. Since beauty is a product of artistic play, we understand the deeper meaning of Schiller's claim in the *Ninth Letter* that the key to the gates of progress is Fine Art.

In the *Eighteenth Letter* Schiller points out that if beauty brings the senses nearer to reason and reason nearer the senses, it follows "dass es zwischen Materie und Form, zwischen Leiden und Tätigkeit einen mittleren Zustand geben müsse, und dass uns die Schönheit in diesen *mittleren* Zustand versetze" ("that there must be a state midway between matter and form, passivity and activity, and that it is into this *middle* state that beauty transports us"). He calls this middle condition the aesthetic state. He distinguishes between an aesthetic state as political organization (*Staat*) and as an individual state of mind (*Zustand*).

C Semblance and the Aesthetic State

Schiller's aim in the last section is to enlarge upon the role of art in social evolution and in everyday living. His thesis is that real human progress is toward the aesthetic state. He says that the aesthetic state is the natural object of the drive to play. He observes that we are transported into this ideal condition through the enjoyment and through the creation of various kinds of "aesthetic semblance" (*ästhetischer Schein*).

In the *Twenty-Sixth Letter* Schiller defines two kinds of semblance. False semblance (*falscher Schein*) is always deceptive; it misleads judgment because it pretends to mirror reality. Human beings practice false semblance, for instance, when they pretend to be something they are not. Artistic semblance applies only to art, and it is what distinguishes art from reality. Art as aesthetic semblance is man-made and independent of reality. Since aesthetic semblance pretends to be nothing other than it is, there is no danger of confusing it with truth and reality: "den Schein der ersten Art für etwas gelten lassen, kann der Wahrheit niemals Eintrag tun, weil man nie Gefahr läuft, ihn derselben unterzuschieben, was doch die einzige Art ist, wie der Wahrheit geschadet werden kann" ("To attach value to semblance . . . can never be prejudicial to truth, because one is never in danger of substituting it for truth, which is after all the only way in which truth can ever be impaired," XXVI, 5.) For Schiller, a work of art is pure illusion. Like a rainbow or a sunset it is devoid of substance and has no separate reality apart from its appearance. Herein lies its power. Since artistic semblance cannot be used for anything, the mind is liberated from practical considerations; and it slips out of the everyday world into the realm of sheer appearance—which is the aesthetic state. Semblance, therefore, is the instrument which transports us from reality into aesthetic freedom.

The aesthetic state itself is a modality of the psyche which we can involve in our everyday life and in our moral activities from the most trivial to the most noble. It is an ideal pattern of personal behavior which elevates us above what we are doing; for example, nature does not care if we practice good table manners so long as we satisfy the appetite. Likewise, it makes no difference to moral necessity how we do what we have to do. But it makes a great deal of difference to our status as human beings. Because whenever we adorn an act with beauty, we free ourselves. Free, because we decide when, where, and how the action will be performed, and because we no longer act in accordance with blind necessity but in accordance with the aesthetic form we give it. Whenever we do more than necessity dictates, we transcend necessity—which is the definition of aesthetic freedom.

According to Schiller, aesthetic semblance has always played the leading role in mankind's rise from barbarism. No matter how far back we go in history, we observe that as soon as man satisfies his material needs he displays "die Freude am *Schein*, die Neigung zum *Putz* und zum *Spiele*" ("a delight in *semblance*, and a propensity to *ornamentation* and *play*," XXVI, 3). Schiller constructs the scenario of past progress: man on the lowest level dedicates himself exclusively to accumulating the necessities of survival. Once he feels secure, he commences to notice the external appearance of his possessions. Eventually dissatisfied with the utilitarian virtues of his goods, he wants them to please the eye as well. This explains why the ancient German went after glossier hides and why the warrior decorated his sword. Man ornaments his possessions for the same reason that he plays. Second, man adorns himself with jewelry and decorates his house. Yet he does not rest content even here. No longer satisfied that only his possessions give pleasure, he desires that *he* please as well. Thus, third, he transfers the visual quality of his goods to the way he acts. He lends his gestures and his speech a playful elegance, an artistic grace that delights the eye and the ear while informing the mind. Social grace is of paramount importance in Schiller's system of everyday living because, since social grace and artistic semblance are identical, we dwell in the aesthetic condition when we cultivate them.

We are now in a position to understand the relation between the physical, the aesthetic, and the moral states: in the physical state the appetites rule man one-sidedly. It is infinitely difficult to move from there to the aesthetic state because that requires a complete transformation of character. The aesthetic state denotes the harmonious interaction of the *Stofftrieb* and the *Formtrieb*. The moral state is one of rational preponderance into which the individual can move when circumstances so require. Schiller emphasizes that we can reach this high level only from the aesthetic state. The transition is easy because both conditions are rooted in disinterested activity. As aesthetic enjoyment is its own reward, so is the pure moral act. Even though the moral state ranks higher on the scale of achievement, the aesthetic condition is better because it involves balance.

This concludes the discussion of Schiller's essay. We have seen how he investigates the relationship of art and beauty to life, to politics, and to social evolution. The chief idea underlying the essay is that both individual and social progress is possible. Since he believes that the social system emanates from the character of its citizens, the individual can improve society only by improving himself first. The reason why the eighteenth century finds itself unable to take another step forward is because the citizen's animal and rational drives have been put into an adversary relationship. The drives can be made to work in unison again by the systematic cultivation of the drive to play. Since the natural product of play is aesthetic semblance—beauty—and since aesthetic semblance is the instrument which transports us to the aesthetic state, we can have progress by educating the faculty for appreciating and for creating beauty, *taste*.

Reduced to a single statement, Schiller's theory of progress could be stated as follows: if man surrounds himself with beauty, and adorns his thoughts and deeds with playful elegance, he will improve not only his own character but also society as a whole.

II   On Naive and Sentimental Poetry

Schiller began work on the essay *On Naive and Sentimental Poetry* while he was still involved with the *Aesthetic Letters*. The essay elaborates on the human condition with the object of explaining why there are basically two modes of perceiving the world, two kinds of human temperament, two kinds of moral behavior, two varieties of art, and why there are realists and idealists.

The structure of the following exposition reflects the divisions which Schiller made in the essay when serializing it in his literary journal *Die Horen*. "Über das Naive" appeared in the eleventh issue of 1795. The twelfth issue of 1795 contains "Die sentimental-ischen Dichter". The third part appeared in the first issue of 1796 and bore the title "Beschluss der Abhandlung über naive und sentimentalische Dichter, nebst einigen Bemerkungen einen karak-teristischen Unterschied unter den Menschen betreffend" [Conclusion of the Treatise On Naive and Sentimental Poetry Together with some Observations Concerning a Characteristic Difference Among Men].

Following Schiller's pattern, the first main section of the following discussion elucidates through literary examples the characteristics of the naive and the varieties of naive moral behavior. The second section concerns his views on naive and sentimental poetry, while the third concentrates on Schiller's conception of what constitutes a realist and an idealist.

A   *The Naive*

Schiller begins with the observation that as children we begin life in a state of oneness with nature and with ourselves. Since as children we believe the world to be exactly as it appears to us, we accept it for what it is and relate directly to it—instinctively and automatically. In the early years of our lives we are unaware that appearances are often deceptive and that a separate reality often exists beyond them. We do not know that adults can pretend to be what they are not. Nor do we know that it is possible to speak other than the truth. As children we are easily duped. We believe whatever anybody tells us. We are innocent, artless, simple, unpretentious, honest, straightforward, trusting, unsophisticated, naive. Shakespeare says it more eloquently when in *Richard III* Gloucester addresses the young Prince of Wales: "Sweet prince, the untainted virtue of years hath not yet dived into the world's deceit: No more can you distinguish of a man than his outward show; which, God he knows, seldom or never jumpeth with the heart" (III,1). In moral behavior, the naive individual seems to do the right thing automatically and spontaneously, as if nature were whispering directions into his ear.

We do not remain in this condition of pristine innocence any longer than it takes our parents to teach us the forms and laws of society. Strict limitations are set upon what we do and say and to how we do and say it. When we begin to live according to rules instead of instinct, we sever ourselves from nature. We also split the heart from the mind. With nature no longer to guide us, we must reflect upon our decisions. Our behavior is no more the spontaneous expression of unity, but the result of calculation and choice. We become artful, sophisticated, knowledgeable, reflective, civilized, sentimental. Schiller uses the word "sentimental" in its older meaning to signify intellectual, speculative activity. Schiller goes on to observe that as adults we know the advantages of concealing our true feelings behind a mask. We learn to misrepresent the truth from fear of pain or for motive of gain. As we become more and more skilled at false semblance, we gradually create a phantom self, an alter ego, capable of saying and doing things quite different from what we really are. Hiding behind the mask is dangerous because, in accordance with the mimetic impulse, we run the risk of becoming what we pretend to be. Unlike aesthetic semblance, which we practice for its own sake, false semblance always involves a secondary motive.

Schiller's main objective in the first section is to examine the types of moral behavior that emanate from uncorrupted nature, and to describe the manner in which sentimental man perceives, and reacts to, such behavior.

Having lost our own naiveness, we experience a special sensation when we observe it in others, particularly in children. When a child enters a fashionable soirée and unknowingly breaks a convention, everyone laughs good-naturedly. At the same time we experience melancholy and feel a little ashamed—but not for the sake of broken convention, Schiller says. Rather, it is the idea of our own lost unity mediated by the child that makes us feel that way. For what we are observing on a higher level is pure human nature untainted by civilization. Whenever we see natural harmony and false semblance side by side, when we observe how the former unmasks the latter, and when we know that nature is right and artifice wrong, it makes us feel good. Schiller calls this sensation moral pleasure.

There are two kinds of moral pleasure that result from two kinds of naive behavior: that which is unplanned and that which results from temperament. Each evokes a different response from the spectator.

The first kind of naive behavior is called *das Naive der Überraschung* ("the naive of surprise"). It applies only to the sentimental person who is pretending to be something he is not and also only when he is caught off guard. It is simply the instinctive reaction to the unexpected. For example, as a loud crash behind our backs makes us flinch involuntarily, so a sudden turn of events can precipitate a reflex action from our character that uncovers the part of us which we want to conceal. Hypothetically, we might pretend admiration for someone whom we actually despise, then reveal our true feelings under stress. In every case the true self shines through for all to see. When we finally regain our senses, we are shocked at our behavior. It is not to our personal credit either that nature has been vindicated through us because it has happened against our will. The pleasure which the spectator experiences at such a sight is of two sorts. He feels amused at our expense, and he enjoys the moral pleasure of seeing nature triumph over pretension. Dostoevsky provides a good example of spontaneous moral behavior in Katerina Ivanovna's performance at Dmitri Karamazov's trial for his father's murder in *The Brothers Karamazov* (1881).

Katerina's hysterical outburst and testimony which convicts Dmitri is the long delayed reaction to the way he humiliated her about a year before the action of the novel begins. During that year, she succeeded in concealing her hatred and her thirst for revenge from everyone, deluding even herself. But finally, during her testimony at the trial, an unexpected turn of events provokes the reflex action associated with surprise and allows us to see the real Katerina behind the mask.

During the first part of her testimony, she had projected the image of the chaste maiden sacrificing her own reputation in a selfless effort to moderate Dmitri's sentence. Suddenly Ivan, whom she loves without admitting it to herself, bursts into court to declare that it was Smerdyakov and not Dmitri who killed their father, and that he, Ivan, put him up to it. She is stunned to see the man she loves sacrificing himself for the man she loathes. The surprise triggers the expression of her true feelings. In a fit of uncontrolled hysteria she vents upon Dmitri her pent-up hatred and her craving for revenge. She denounces him as the murderer and produces the evidence that convicts him. Dostoevsky's comment on the scene can serve as the definition for naive behavior provoked by surprise: "The moment of revenge had come upon her suddenly, and all that had been accumulating so long and so painfully . . . burst out all at once and unexpectedly. She betrayed Mitya, but she betrayed herself, too. And no sooner had she given full expression to her feelings than the tension of course was over and she was overwhelmed with shame."[4]

The reader's response to Katerina's behavior has all the ingredients which Schiller specifies. In the first place, we experience the malicious pleasure that always attends catching someone in a lie. If the consequences of her actions were not so tragic, we would also feel amused at her expense. In the second place, we do not admire her for this act because it occurs against her will. It frightens her and causes great regret. Nor do we respect her true feelings once revealed because they are disfigured by wounded vanity. What we admire and what gives us pleasure is the sight of nature and truth winning over artifice and false semblance: "Denn die Natur im Gegensatz gegen die Künstelei und die Wahrheit im Gegensatz gegen den Betrug muss jederzeit Achtung erregen. Wir empfinden also auch über das Naive der Überraschung ein wirklich moralisches Vergnügen"[5] ("For nature in contrast with artifice and truth in contrast with deceit must always engender respect. We therefore experience a truly moral pleasure even at the expense of the naive of surprise").

In addition to naive behavior provoked by surprise, there is naive behavior that arises from temperament. As spectators, we not only experience the moral pleasure of seeing genuineness triumphant, we also honor the person as moral object. In both types of behavior nature kills falsehood, but when it emanates from temperament the credit for the victory goes to the individual because his actions are the direct expression of a personality at one with itself.

The naive hero is not new to literature. In earlier German literature we see him as Parzival and as Simplicissimus. More recently in Goethe's *Egmont* where the protagonist walks into the duke of Alba's trap, or when Wilhelm Tell gets himself locked up for naively telling the Vogt that the second arrow was meant for his lordship. The heroine of La Motte-Fouquet's *Undine* along with Goethe's Mignon are also sometimes used to exemplify the naive temperament. In French literature, Voltaire's Candide, Balzac's Eugéne de Rastignac, Maupassant's Bel Ami, and Marcel Pagnol's Topaz likewise tell the story of a naive hero who is either destroyed or who learns to dissemble. Now despite the fact that in most cases the author is using the naive hero to uncover the insincerities of his generation, rather frequently deception appears in a positive light. Egmont and Wilhelm Tell are tainted in this way because, however much we excuse their actions by calling them naive and despite our admiration for their noble simplicity, we cannot help thinking that they should know better. Nor can it be argued without elaborate qualification that nature is triumphing over artifice. More often than not it is the other way around. Egmont is executed, Mignon dies, Tell lies in order to be able to escape from Gessler's ship and then plots his death. Eugéne de Rastignac can hardly wait to throw off the burden of his innocence, and Topaz becomes highly skilled in deception and dies rich.

To my knowledge, there are only two instances in literature which fully sustain Schiller's conception of the naive temperament while at the same time presenting it as desirable: Prince Myshkin in Dostoevsky's *The Idiot* (1874) and Alyosha Karamazov in *The Brothers Karamazov*. In both novels, the heroes grow up isolated from society, uncontaminated by civilized wants. Consequently, they still possess that original innocence and inner unity when they enter the world of sham. When Myshkin joins Petersburg society, he finds it peopled with rapacious fortune hunters, swindlers, pompous nobodies, malicious slanderers, and tortured misfits of every kind. He does not melt into that society but like a sore finger, becomes the center of attention. Although Myshkin is aware of traditional material values and social conventions, he is indifferent to them. Since he has only a hazy conception of what he himself is, he does not fully understand when his friends love, hate, and fear him all at the same time. But the readers know. Myshkin constantly keeps the image of the ideal before their eyes, reminding them of what they once were and of their potential to be likewise. He involuntarily shows them how shabby they look beside him, and this exposes their insincerity. He reflects pure, they disfigured nature; he is real, they are artificial; he is right, and they are tragically wrong.

Dostoevsky considered Myshkin a limited success because the novel does not consistently evoke the right response from the reader. Quite often Myshkin seems inadequately equipped for life. His friends systematically cheat and deceive him. Finally, unable to cope with the ordeal of Nastasya's murder, he relapses into insanity. We are left with the feeling that an outrageous injustice has been perpetrated, that nature has been wrongfully defeated. A naive person in the best sense of the word, by comparison, should evoke in us intense satisfaction that nature rightfully prevails. We should feel something like admiration and honor for what he is, and a longing for the ideal which he represents. Alyosha Karamazov meets all the requirements because he has, in addition to Myshkin's qualities of naive temperament, a more assertive will and a good knowledge of social survival techniques. Though he is not as colorfully drawn as the rest of the Karamazov family, the novel flows in his direction. Everyone in the book gradually subordinates himself to Alyosha until, at the very end, it is he who dominates the action and gives the orders.

B   The Sentimental Poets

If the poet exists integrally he will produce naive art, which we recognize by three characteristics: the poet's mode of perception, his mode of expression, and his spontaneity. According to Schiller, there is something mechanical about the way naive poets like Homer, Shakespeare, and Goethe write. It seems as if they merely transcribe what some inner voice dictates. Sentimental poets like Schiller, on the other hand, have to sweat out every word. Since they are split off from nature, their mode of perception has changed and they must create by conscious effort.

The naive poet believes the world to be exactly as he perceives it. Consequently, he accepts it and describes it for what it is, whereas the sentimental poet must first filter his perceptions through the ideal. Schiller says that his greatest difficulty in reading the naive poets lay in his habit of separating the author from his work. Educated on sentimental fare, Schiller was trained to look for the author somewhere outside the work so as to read and to reflect along with him. Finally, he realized that in naive poetry it is not possible to separate the man from his work. The poet is the work and vice versa. Divided within himself, the sentimental writer creates impersonally, from the outside.

Schiller illustrates the difference between the naive and the sentimental modes of perception by comparing the way Homer and Ariosto react to the spectacle of principles winning over passion: In book 6 of *The Iliad* Glaucus and Diomedes meet in battle. While Glaucus recites his pedigree, Diomedes realizes that before the war their fathers had been friends. So he suggests that they too honor the ancient rules of hospitality, make friends, and agree to stay out of each other's way for the rest of the war. They exchange armor as a token of their agreement. Homer describes this event as a commonplace, as if it were the most natural thing in the world to do. His matter-of-fact, purely descriptive style reflects his naive mode of perception.

If spontaneous moral behavior is the exception, as it is today, then the author's tone will be flavored with admiration. In his *Orlando Furioso*, Ariosto comes near to swooning in inarticulate awe when Ferrau, the Saracen, and Rinaldo, the Christian, stop their fighting, make friends, and mount the same horse to pursue the fleeing Angelica. Ariosto admires the event because it is the exception, thus exemplifying the sentimental mode of perception. Schiller goes on to say that the Greek as a person of naive temperament relates directly to the object, to the person, or to the event. He does not step outside of himself to observe himself and his work from a distance. His divided descendant, on the other hand, must relate the object to his mind's image of the ideal before he can experience the feeling. When the sentimental man looks at a horse, for instance, he filters his perception of it through the ideal of horseness, then relates to the horse on that basis. The reverse is true for the naive individual.

There are three kinds of sentimental literature that are filtered through the mind. If the poet compares his image of the ideal with reality and saddens at the discrepancy, his language will be flavored with derision and ridicule—the classic components of satire. If he focuses more acutely on the ideal and bemoans its loss, his language will be colored with nostalgia and lament—the classic components of the elegy.

Every sentimental poet will perceive and write in one of these two modes until such time as the ideal and reality coincide. Then his language will be filled with praise and exclamations of satisfaction—the classic components of the sentimental idyl.

Schiller says that the purpose of the sentimental idyl "ist überall nur der, den Menschen im Stand der Unschuld, d. h. in einem Zustand der Harmonie und des Friedens mit sich selbst und von aussen darzustellen" ("is invariably to represent man in a state of innocence, i.e. in a condition of harmony and of peace with himself and with his environment," XII, 223). Properly speaking, the sentimental idyl is the art form of the Golden Age, though it could, theoretically, appear earlier if the poet knew how to purge himself of patterned thinking. Schiller doubts that a contemporary could write such an account, because in a highly developed society man can no more avoid learning its values, customs, and traditions than he can avoid growing up and learning how to speak. Men are prisoners of their age.

Schiller does not know of any contemporary work which is a total realization of what he has in mind. There are limited successes like Gessler's idyls, portions of Klopstock's _Messiah_, here and there in Thomson's _Seasons_, and in Hölderlin's poetry. To my knowledge, the only modern German author to employ this art form with considerable success is Günter Grass in _The Tin Drum_ (1959). Underlying that novel is a familiar three phase progression from innocence through guilt toward an ideal synthesis. Significantly, Oskar is born civilized with all of his faculties developed, knowing and wise, yet innocent. His first sensation in the world is nausea at the prospect of growing up as his father's apprentice, getting married, inheriting the family store, and spending Sundays at grandmother's. His decision to stop growing and speaking at the age of three immunizes him from social forces. Free, process-oriented, and satisfied with himself and the world, Oskar cultivates the inner balance. He teaches himself to read from two books, _Rasputin and His Women_ and Goethe's _Elective Affinities_. The first symbolizes flesh, the second spirit. He tears the pages from each book, then shuffles them together like a deck of playing cards, signifying fusion. Midway through the novel he chooses to lose his innocence and enters the second stage where he stops playing and starts working. He joins the multitude for whom effort is separated from reward, means from ends. Accordingly, he turns into a grotesque dwarf and begins to converse. After several years of guilt, alienation, and inner conflict, he emerges into the third stage, where once again he is a unity—but on a higher level, as he attains the innocence that accompanies the harmonious admixture of inno-cence, knowledge, and experience. Although the world is disjointed, Oskar forgives it because he knows that imbalance is a stage that every human and that every society must traverse. Oskar's only deviation from the progression is that, recognizing the inevitability of progress, he makes it an object of free choice and therefore transcends it.

Oskar's direct mode of perceiving the world and his poetic representation of it reflect the tone of the sentimental idyl. Oskar never moralizes about the events portrayed; rather, he tells the stories in a style quite similar to that of the naive poets. He discusses vanilla pudding, a way to fish for eels, death by strangulation, love and disappointment—all with the same matter of factness. At the end of the novel Oskar is presented as having attained the ideal, however grotesquely.

Now that Schiller has explored the features of the naive and the sentimental, he converts his theory of poetry into a general theory of mankind: Subtract the poetic dimension from what he has been saying about naive and sentimental poets and we have the realist and the idealist—the two basic kinds of people there are in the world. To be sure, there is no such thing as a pure realist totally devoid of reason or an idealist who has no heart, he says. In reality, each partakes of the other. But when viewed as a whole, men lean toward one or the other extreme.

C   The Realist and the Idealist

The difference between the realist and the idealist is the same as that between the naive and the sentimental poets, between animal man and rational man. They represent two fundamentally different ways of perceiving the world, two sources of knowledge, two value systems, and two types of moral behavior. This explains to Schiller why no one can please universally. Because when he evokes the acclaim of one group, he automatically incurs the wrath of the other. Schiller's analysis clarifies the problem and offers a solution.

1.   The Realist

The realist is grounded in nature. Having no preconceived notions of perfectibility, he accepts the world exactly as it is. His knowledge and his rules for living derive from observation and experience, not from speculation. Observation tells him two things about nature. When viewed as a totality, it works consistently according to universal principles. But not so in specific cases. Nature is composed of individual parts which interact with one another and with circumstance in a mutually dependent relationship. In specific cases nature is unfree, intertwined, and limited. Accordingly, the realist practices situation ethics; that is, he adapts his judgment and behavior to the context. This explains why, for example, King Philip II in *Don Carlos* can pardon Medina Sidonia for losing the Spanish Armada, telling him that he sent his ships against men, not against storms. The realist is consequently fair-minded and tolerant.

The realist displays his *Weltanschauung* in all his thoughts and actions. His life is like a well-planned garden in which everything has a value beyond its immediate existence. He appraises according to usefulness. That something might possess its value within itself is inconceivable to him. He only wants to know what it is good *for*. Thus the object of his morality is the practical, the beneficial, and the useful. Whomever he loves, he enjoys making glad with gifts. In matters of politics, he aims at the greatest good for the greatest number.

The realist is better suited to life than the idealist because he swims with the current. Yet, at the same time, he is limited by what gives him his strength. Experience teaches only what is valid under certain conditions and what must happen for something else to happen. Since he does not cultivate the rational faculty, he does not see beyond the world of sense. He lacks vision. His actions are determined by outside forces and by external purposes. What he is and does is not the result of free choice but of submission to necessity. He sees and judges man, for instance, only as he appears in his present, imperfect reality rather than in his infinite potential. Change, progress, freedom, and absolutes are figments and belief in them not much better than fanaticism.

The characteristics of the realist are even more noticeable in caricature. The false realist resembles Schiller's description, in the *Twenty-Third Letter*, of man in a state of savagery. Instead of submitting to the necessity of nature as a whole, he submits himself indiscriminately to it as a blind force. Consequently, he is the victim of every wild impulse. He knows only what his eyes and his ears tell him. He values only what satisfies his appetites. Unthinking and unaware, he lives in servitude to chance and circumstance.

2. *The Idealist*

The perverted extreme of idealism is equally striking. The false idealist, or fanatic, cuts himself off not only from nature but also from moral law in general, not in order to strive for something better, but "um dem Eigensinne der Begierden und den Launen

der Einbildungskraft desto ungebundener nachgeben zu können"
("So as to better indulge the wantoness of his desires and the whims
of his imagination," XIII, 263). He renounces nature, moral
constraint, and the very concept of character. He declares for law-
lessness. Still, this caricature emanates from something infinitely
perfectible.

The true idealist is quite different from the fanatic. He has
separated himself from nature because reason tells him that he
cannot find in nature the eternal principles that he seeks. His
freedom is the kind we recognize from his essay on aesthetics, where
it means liberation *from* transitoriness and blind impulse *to* create
what is enduring. Here is the chief difference between the realist
and the idealist. Grounded in nature, the realist is determined by
the necessity of nature and limited by condition. Grounded in
reason, the idealist subjects the world to rational principles and so
imposes the character of independence on whatever he does.

The idealist derives his knowledge and his rules for living from
reason. Since he has preconceived notions of perfectibility, he does
not take the world—or people—for what it is, but as the ideal tells
him it could be. Thus, he evaluates people according to their
potential for approximating the ideal, not as they are in imperfect
reality. This explains why the idealist is often unfair and intolerant.

We observe the idealist's attitude throughout his daily activities.
Nonutilitarian, he appraises according to worth. He wants to know
whether a person or a thing is good, not what it is good *for*. Unlike
the realist, he lays out his garden on a grand scale with little regard
for practicalities. His moral decisions are oriented toward the
unconditioned and the absolute. Whomever he loves he ennobles.
In political matters his object is freedom. What he is and does is the
result of free choice. He rejects situation ethics in favor of universals.
When his actions are viewed as a whole, he displays no uniformity,
simply because consistency and freedom are opposites.

Concluding the exposition of Schiller's essay, we see that the poet
views man as split between two opposing tendencies. The one is
grounded in nature, the other in reason. Neither alone is sufficient
for us to experience what it means to be human. The ideal, of
course, involves the synthesis of the two extremes in which the
realist is brought nearer to reason and the idealist integrates feeling.
In this way a balance could be established. Neither side would
infringe on the territory of the other but instead both would serve as
a source of mutual stimulation.

III   *The Sublime*

I will conclude my exposition of Schiller's theoretical writings with a brief look at the close relationship between his concept of sublimity, the fundamental idea of his classical drama, and his philosophical speculations about moral behavior. In his essays *Über das Pathetische* [On Suffering] and *Über das Erhabene* [On Sublimity] he says that in the aesthetic condition reason and feeling accord. In the sublime, they collide. The rational is always dominant and feeling always agonizes. We can define sublimity as ideal moral behavior despite great suffering. A sublime victory occurs whenever in life or upon the stage moral principles clash with and defeat such deterministic forces as inclination, circumstance, fate, or when one moral law is sacrificed for a law of higher value. The following remarks are meant to clarify this idea.

In his essay on suffering, Schiller distinguishes between two kinds of pure moral behavior which we call sublime. *"Passive sublimity"* (*das Erhabene der Fassung*) occurs when we submit cheerfully to a misfortune which we cannot avoid. The passively sublime hero allows adversity to change neither his values nor his outlook on life because he operates according to the principle that "eine Gewalt . . . *dem Begriff nach zu vernichten,* heisst aber nichts anders, als sich derselben freiwillig unterwerfen" (*"to destroy the very concept* of a force means simply to submit to it voluntarily," XII, 266.) As an example, Schiller cites the Jew Nathan in Lessing's drama *Nathan der Weise* (1779). In that play, Nathan loses everything he owns and nearly everyone he loves. He is crushed beneath prejudice, malevolence, and circumstance. Yet he continues to act like a man without a care in the world because he accepts his fate voluntarily.

In "active sublimity" (*das Erhabene der Handlung*), the anguish is always the product of a free choice. There are, in turn, two kinds of active sublimity, moral and aesthetic. In a morally sublime act a person chooses to act according to principles even though he knows that he will suffer for his decision, that it may even cost his life. Schiller uses Leonidas at Thermopylae to illustrate this point. Though he and the three hundred Spartans had a chance to escape with their lives, they fought to the last man in obedience to duty. Schiller calls Leonidas's deed morally sublime because "sein Leiden ist eine *Willenshandlung"* ("his suffering is *an act of will,"* XI, 264).

The second type of active sublimity involves a crime against oneself. The idea works as follows. As human beings we act according to a personal code of ethics which make us what we are. Although we may be willing to compromise our values to a point, there is a line which we cannot force ourselves to cross. But it happens on occasion that we accidentally or through some error in judgment overstep that line—which means that we violate ourselves. Whether another person is involved or not is immaterial because the perpetrator is the real victim. The remorse is so intense that it drives us to inflict pain on ourselves in expiation. We endure the pain gladly because it extinguishes the sense of remorse. Suffering purifies because when we reach the summit of misery the old self perishes and a new one takes its place. If, for example, Leonidas had shirked his duty then punished himself in remorse, his suffering would be *aesthetically* sublime. Aesthetic sublimity, therefore, consists of four stages in a definite sequence: (1) crime, (2) guilt, (3) punishment, (4) renewal. The transformation itself happens "nicht allmählich (denn es gibt von der Abhängigkeit keinen Übergang zur Freiheit), sondern plötzlich und durch eine Erschütterung reisst es den selbständigen Geist aus dem Netze los, womit die verfeinerte Sinnlichkeit ihn umstrickte" ("not gradually [for there is no transition from dependence to freedom], but suddenly and with a shock it tears the independent spirit out of the net in which refined sensuousnesss has entoiled it," XII, 272). In short, an aesthetically sublime act is one of self-creation in accordance with moral principles.

Of the two kinds of active sublimity, the morally sublime is superior because the hero suffers rather than violates principles, which is ideal behavior. The aesthetically sublime act is always performed because of the remorse engendered by breaking one's own moral law. The morally sublime hero behaves ideally, whereas the aesthetically sublime hero becomes the ideal. For this reason, the latter is more suitable for tragedy simply because the spectacle of emotional turmoil, agonizing choices, crime and punishment, freedom and spiritual rebirth gives greater aesthetic pleasure than the presentation of a virtuous man steadfastly obeying the law.

Let us illustrate the stages of aesthetic sublimity by showing how Dostoevsky handles it in *Crime and Punishment* (1866). The hero of the novel, Raskolnikov, kills a malicious old woman to discover what kind of person he is. If afterward he feels indifferent, he will know that he is like Napoleon, Julius Caesar, and other great men of history who distinguished themselves, among other things, by their apparent ability to break laws with a clear conscience. If, on the other hand, Raskolnikov comes away with feelings of guilt, then he will know that he is "a louse like everybody else who does not have the right to step over barriers."[6] The experiment is vain if for no other reason than that a great man would never doubt himself in such a manner. So it comes as no surprise that for two weeks after the murder Raskolnikov experiences the agony of remorse. He loses faith in himself and in life, not because he killed but because he proved to himself that he was not a great man. All he has succeeded in proving is that "I am an aesthetic louse and nothing more."[7] Existence finally becomes so painful that he confesses everything to the police. For he knows that if he is ever to regain peace of mind, he must expiate the crime. He is sentenced to eight years of hard labor in Siberia. A few months after his arrival there and after more suffering, he experiences a transformation from which he emerges renewed. It occurs suddenly as specified: "How it happened he did not know. But all at once something seemed to seize him and fling him at Sonia's feet. He wept and threw his arms round her knees. . . . At last the moment had come."[8] As the novel begins with Raskolnikov's spiritual death, it ends with his rebirth.

There are many examples of sublimity in Schiller's dramas: when Karl Moor surrenders to the police, when Mary Stuart and Joan of Arc are punished for crimes of which they are innocent, and when Don Cesar in *Die Braut von Messina* kills himself to expiate his brother's murder. I will comment on their sublime activities in my discussion of the individual plays.

CHAPTER 2

Poetry

SCHILLER'S poetry readily lends itself to division into three
periods. The first coincides with his youth. Through grandilo-
quent rhetoric and emotional excesses, his style reflects the flamboy-
ance so characteristic of the *Sturm und Drang* movement. The
middle period covers the years 1785 to 1789. Here a different
Schiller speaks. The poems incline toward philosophical ideas, and
the language is restrained and elevated. Between 1789 and 1795
Schiller did not write a single poem. In the first years of the interval
he spent his time preparing his lectures for the university. Later he
studied Kant and wrote his essays on history and aesthetics. During
this time, he underwent a transformation culminating in a spiritual
and artistic renewal. His subsequent works have the ring of the self-
confident master.

What kind of poetry did Schiller write? Was he a poet who wrote
philosophy or a philosopher who wrote poetry? He was both.
Schiller was by no means enamored of this duality. In a letter to
Goethe dated 31 August 1794 he complains that when he is writing
poetry the philosopher often gets in the way, and when he is
philosophizing the poet catches him unawares. Owing to this
admixture of imagination and speculation, Schiller is not a lyrical
poet in the narrow sense. Pure lyrical poetry is almost always a
subjective account of the poet's feelings and sensations. Its appeal
lies mainly in the masterful use of the poetic forms, in the excellence
of expression, and in its closeness to our own sensations. Like music,
it is often enjoyed for its own sake. Schiller, however, is not content
with delighting the ear. He also wants to inform the mind. Consequently, most of what he wrote is crystallized around an idea. The
Germans call this blend of lyrics and thought *Gedankenlyrik*.

Schiller believes that the mission of the poet is to improve the
reader's mind. In the *Ninth Letter* he says the poet should impart to
the world a direction toward the good and the ideal: "An ihrem

Müssiggange kannst du deine bildende Hand versuchen. . . . Wo du sie findest, umgib sie mit edeln, mit grossen, mit geistreichen Formen, schliesse sie ringsum mit den Symbolen des Vortrefflichen ein, bis der Schein die Wirklichkeit und die Kunst die Natur überwindet" ("On their leisure hours you can try your shaping hand. . . . Surround them wherever you meet them, with the great and noble forms of genius, and encompass them [about] with the symbols of perfection, until Semblance conquer reality and art triumph over nature." Schiller rarely deviates from this aim.

Schiller's characteristic mode of expression is the grand style. He draws upon the widest range of literature, philosophy, and history. He emphasizes the ultimate questions about the good, the true, and the beautiful. His subjects are the fate of civilizations, the destiny of nations, man's involvement in the world theater. The language of his early period displays the delight in rhetorical embellishment characteristic of the baroque. His later style, by contrast, is simple, dynamic, and lofty. In reading Schiller one is always aware of his basic technique: magnification. Through metaphor and allusion he expands his subject until it provides a panorama of the universe and all that is human. Consequently, we have the sensation of undergoing an elevating experience. There is no better illustration of Schiller's mature style than the elegy *Nänie* (1799).

Auch das Schöne muss sterben! Das Menschen und Götter bezwinget,
  Nicht die eherne Brust rüht es des stygischen Zeus.
Einmal nur erweichte die Liebe den Schattenbeherrscher,
  Und an der Schwelle noch, streng, rief er zurück sein Geschenk.
Nicht stillt Aphrodite dem schönen Knaben die Wunde,
  Die in den zierlichen Leib grausam der Eber geritzt.
Nicht errettet den göttlichen Held die unsterbliche Mutter,
  Wann er, am skäischen Tor fallend, sein Schicksal erfüllt.
Aber sie steigt aus dem Meer mit allen Töchtern des Nereus,
  Und die Klage hebt an um den verherrlichten Sohn.
Siehe! Da weinen die Götter, es weinen die Göttinnen alle,
  Dass das Schöne vergeht, dass das Vollkommene stirbt.
Auch ein Klaglied zu sein im Mund der Geliebten, ist herrlich,
  Denn das Gemeine geht klanglos zum Orkus hinab.[1]

Even beauty must perish! What subdues gods and humans
  Has no effect on the iron bosom of Stygian Zeus.
Only once was softened by love the sovereign of shadows,
  But on the threshold's step, ruthless, the gift he recalled.
Aphrodite fails to stanch the wound of her lover,

Savagely carved by the boar into his comely shape.
Rescue can't the immortal mother her god-like hero,
  As at the Scaean gate falling, his fate he fulfills.
But from the sea she rises with all the daughters of Nereus,
  And she starts the lament for her immortalized son.
See there, the gods are now weeping, all goddesses weep now together
  That the beautiful, too, dies, that perfection must pass.
Also to be a mourning song sung by a lover is heavenly,
  For the common sinks soundless to Orkus below.[2]

The poem laments the fact that everything is transitory, even beauty perishes. Neither the gods nor mortal man can prevent its death. The power of Orpheus' music, the erotic love of Aphrodite, and Thetis' maternal concern are unable to make beauty eternal. But though beauty perishes in the physical world, it attains immortality in man's mind through art.

The structure of the poem implies what the content expresses. It is written in elegiac distichs, which is the ancient elegiac form consisting of a hexameter followed by a pentameter. Schiller himself gives a description of it: "Im Hexameter steigt des Springquells flüssige Säule, / Im Pentameter drauf fällt sie melodisch ab" ("The hexameter means the fountain's flowing column rises, / In pentameters it sinks melodiously to a stop"). In the poem, the beautiful rises with the hexameter and dies in the pentameter, thereby supporting the opening statement that even beauty must die. Further, the first four distichs set the transitory and the eternal at opposite poles. The dichotomy is emphasized through the skillful manipulation of the caesura. It is marked in the pentameters by the collision of two stressed syllables which force a pause. On one side is life and beauty, on the other is pain and death: "Die in den zierlichen Leib // grausam der Eber geritzt." After three distichs beginning with "nicht" and lamenting the demise of beauty, the fifth begins with "aber," introducing the notion that the beautiful does not vanish entirely. This is supported by a subtle modification of the caesura. In the sixth pentameter the poet diminishes the force of the caesura "vergeht, dass," then effaces it almost entirely by the unequal stress of "klánglós." The wavering caesura causes the halves to flow together, thereby signifying that the polarities are reconciled in art. This implies the poem's central idea: although we must accept beauty's inevitable death, it lives forever in art and in the spirit. This view of immortality was that held by the ancient Greeks ever since Homer. They did not believe in life after death.

For them, the worst thing was to die and be forgotten. Eternal life, however, could be achieved by living on in the mind of man through legend and song. Consequently, they strove to live memorable lives.

Nänie also illustrates Schiller's basic technique of magnification. He expands his subject to encompass the great heroes of antiquity, the gods of Olympus, and he ends by revealing the secret of immortality. As the following pages disclose, virtually all his poems share this characteristic. To provide an overall impression of Schiller's poetic muse, I have selected examples from his three main periods. I have categorized them by genre. according to the classification Schiller himself made for the *Prachtausgabe* of his works. To demonstrate his development as a poet, I have arranged the genres chronologically, which he did not do: philosophical poems, elegies, ballads, *Lieder*.

The poems of the first period show a young poet not yet in control of his immense talent. Gradiloquent, emotionally excessive, the poems reflect the subjective attitude toward life of a young man who rebels first and thinks later. Typical of this period is *Der Eroberer* [The Conqueror] written in 1777 at age eighteen. The piece centers around an imaginary tyrant upon whom Schiller vents his hatred of all despots. The first stanza sets the tone for what follows:

> Dir Eroberer, dir schwellet mein Busen auf,
> Dir zu fluchen den Fluch glühnden Rachedursts,
> Vor dem Auge der Schöpfung,
> Vor des Ewigen Angesicht!

> Conqueror, my breast rages to curse you
> With the curse of revenge's glowing thirst,
> Before Creation's eyes,
> Before the Immortal's face!

Continuing in this vein, Schiller depicts the conqueror laying waste the countryside. Villainous and cruel, he ignores the dire effects of his action, for his only concern is to be remembered by posterity as a great warrior. When he dies he ascends with dripping sword to the throne of God to be weighed against his deeds. Proud of his achievements, he sits on one scale while his crimes against humanity are heaped on the other until finally the scales stand exactly even. At this crucial juncture, the poet hurls his curse, which is enough to tip the balance and send the malefactor down to Hell. The ending

of the poem is bizarre in its emotionalism. Ecstatic at the conqueror's demise, the poet thrashes in the dust "jauchzend den Tag,
wo er gerichtet ward" ("rejoicing the day where he was sentenced").

This poem, and others like it, reflect young Schiller's intense
dislike of tyrants, specifically of Duke Karl Eugen. As a youth,
Schiller was an unwilling pupil in the duke's military academy. He
suffered under the harsh discipline and chafed at the petty, sterile
environment. He soon recognized that the school was a reflection of
the duke's character. He was repelled by the duke's arbitrary
despotism, his mediocrity as a man, and his trite preoccupation with
his place in the history books. Ironically, Schiller was one of the
duke's favorites, mainly because he could write impressive verses
celebrating his lordship's magnificence. In his early years, Schiller
had looked forward to these court performances and had enjoyed
being the center of attention. Later, when he was better able to
distinguish between semblance and substance, he turned away. *Der
Eroberer* is a thinly veiled description of his true feelings toward
that ruler.

Schiller's early period came to a close when he moved to Leipzig
at the invitation of Gottfried Körner—a man of wealth, influence,
and taste who admired Schiller. Thanks to Körner's generosity, the
poet was able to apply himself to literary pursuits without financial
worry. Representative of the second period are the philosophical
poems *Resignation* [Resignation], *Die Götter Griechenlandes* [The
Gods of Greece], and *Die Künstler* [The Artists].

Resignation (1785) tells of a man who, after his death, appears
before the judgment seat which is occupied by Eternity. There he
claims his reward for what he believed had been an exemplary life.
He had sacrificed happiness on earth for happiness in the Hereafter.
Now he is returning his unused ticket to happiness:

> Da steh' ich schon auf deiner finstern Brücke,
> Furchtbare Ewigkeit.
> Empfange meinen Vollmachtbrief zum Glücke!
> Ich bring' ihn unerbrochen dir zurücke,
> Ich weiss nichts von Glückseligkeit.

> Already at your somber bridge I tarry,
> Awful eternity.
> Take back my rights to happy life and merry,
> Their seal untouched, to you these rights I carry,
> No, I know nothing of happiness.

He reminds the judge that living a life of abstinence deserves reward, for he gave up his most cherished possession—joy, happiness, even his Laura. In addition, he had to endure the jeers of his fellowmen, who mocked him. With sneering scorn, he relates, they derided his gods as projections of man's fears, as boogeymen who frighten little children, beings who overwhelm the mind where the lamp of knowledge flickers low. Religion is a fraud, they shouted, an ancient piece of mummery sanctified by tradition. Only the cleverness of the camouflage is praiseworthy. For six stanzas Schiller enlarges on this subject, indulging his gift for rhetoric all along the way. For example:

> Was heisst die Zukunft, die uns Gräber decken?
>   Die Ewigkeit, mit der du eitel prangst?
> Ehrwürdig nur, weil Hüllen sie verstecken,
> Der Riesenschatten unsrer eignen Schrecken
>   Im hohlen Spiegel der Gewissensangst.

> What means a future made by tombstones blurry?
>   Life eternal you always harp on, alas?
> Respectful only for the husks they bury,
> That giant shadow of our own worry,
>   The dread of conscience on a hollow glass.

Despite all trials and tribulations, the hero of the poem persevered in his convictions. He has kept his side of the bargain and now he wants to collect:"Vergelterin, ich fordre meinen Lohn." ("Compensator, I demand my reward"). The hero, however, discovers that he has been laboring under a misapprehension. A voice replies that man may choose between two kinds of life. "Sie heissen *Hoffnung* und *Genuss*." ("They're called *hope* and *enjoyment*"). He who picks the one must not covet the other. By *Hoffnung* Schiller means a life oriented toward belief in the Hereafter. He uses *Genuss* in a positive way to mean the doctrine that fulfillment, happiness, and joy in the Present is the sole purpose of existence. You have hoped, the voice says, that is your reward. The poem ends with the observation that whatever we pass up in life will not be waiting for us in eternity:

> Du hast *gehofft*, dein Lohn ist abgetragen,
>   Dein *Glaube* war dein zugewognes Glück.
> Du konntest deine Weisen fragen:
> Was man von der Minute ausgeschlagen,
>   Gibt keine Ewigkeit zurück.

You *hoped,* your wages have been liquidated,
Your *faith,* good fortune for you used to be.
If asked, your wise men might have stated:
What from a minute you eliminated,
Won't be waiting in Eternity.

When Schiller sent this poem to the publisher, he warned that it might run afoul of the censorship and suggested publishing it in another state. Furthermore, he made it clear that the piece was not his *Glaubensbekenntnis* ("confession of faith"). Nevertheless, many readers saw the poem as a thinly veiled attack on the Christian system of values, which is not surprising since it appears that the man makes the sacrifices and endures the abuse for nothing. Eternity rejects his demands and his neighbor laughs at him. Furthermore, this man's fate belies the widespread belief that man can win salvation through good works and abstinence. Still, it is false to read the poem as a *Glaubensbekenntnis* or as an unmasking of the Christian religion. Neither is it a paean to sensual enjoyment nor a celebration of truth and immortality. Rather the poem exposes false virtue which renounces this world for reward in the next. The man of the poem has not comprehended that morality is its own reward. To him, it is a form of delayed gratification, the means to buy his way into Heaven. Morals, Christian or otherwise, practiced with an eye to future gain are worth nothing. In addition, when the man recites the litany of his hardships, he reminds us of the Pharisees of the New Testament who boast and make an ostentatious display of their fasting and mortification. And again, his belief that he has Eternity's promise to compensate him for doing more than is necessary resembles the steward of the parable who had no claim to the thanks of his master and of the workmen in the vineyard (Luke 17:7-10; Matthew 20:1-15). Both parables oppose the calculation of reward for our deeds, deny that man has any claims. Gain cannot serve as the motive of the act, because a good deed with the thought of reward, with an appreciating look at one's achievement, would not be virtue. The actual compensation lies in the good feelings which are aroused by the virtuous deed. This is the significance of the judge's pronouncement that hope was the man's reward and that belief was his happiness. Only he never understood. The poem is therefore not directed against Christian virtues, but questions the value of a deed performed only because the person wants to make a deposit in a celestial savings account to be collected in the Hereafter, with interest.

Schiller spoke the truth when he said that *Resignation* should not be taken for his *Glaubensbekenntnis*. The poem is, however, an expression of his disillusionment with parts of the Christian *Weltanschauung*. His next poem, *Die Götter Griechenlandes* (1788), continues in this vein and states his own views more clearly. In the poem, he praises the Greek system over that of his own age. Schiller knew that his interpretation of the Greeks involved an idealization that never existed in reality: "Schöne Wesen aus dem Fabelland" ("Beautiful creatures from the land of myths"). Based partly on fact and partly on inspiration, Schiller's ancient Greece is a metaphor for man enjoying the pleasure of living at peace with himself and his environment.

There are two versions of the poem. Schiller wrote the first in 1788 in response to Wieland's invitation to contribute to his journal *Der Teutsche Merkur*. Then twenty-nine years old, Schiller was still the angry radical telling people what they did not want to hear. His portrayal of the Enlightenment as a soulless exaltation of reason, and of Christianity as a blight on mankind provoked a loud outcry. Numerous contemporaries called down the wrath of God on the poet. Others criticized his cavalier treatment of historical facts. A few praised it (Wieland, Körner, Goethe, Novalis). In 1793 Schiller wrote a less controversial version deleting the passages which dealt with Christianity. I have chosen the first version for explication because it is more representative of Schiller at this time in his life.

The poem represents the poet as a citizen of the eighteenth century dissatisfied with himself and his culture. He longs for the perfection of ancient Greece. The first ten stanzas celebrate the Greek view of life. It is distinguished above all by its orientation toward man and life. For the Greeks, the meaning of existence resided in this world. Because they animated nature with deities, they enjoyed a sense of intimacy with it. They cultivated the beautiful, ornamenting their goods, themselves, and their language. They even adorned truth with beauty. They did not see the sun rising but the steeds of Helios mounting the sky with flying hoofbeats. They cultivated the spirit and flesh equally, worshipping Apollo and Dionysus with the same enthusiasm:

> Das Evoe muntrer Thyrsusschwinger
> Und der Panther prächtiges Gespann
> Meldeten den grossen Freudebringer,
> Faun und Satyr taumeln ihm voran,
> Um ihn springen rasende Mänaden,
> Ihre Tänze loben seinen Wein.

> Hear the calling of Thyrsus-swingers,
> Him the panthers splendidly bore,
> Announced the mighty Rapturebringer,
> Faun and Satyr tumble before,
> Whirling 'round him raging Maenads,
> Dancing praises to his wine.

They were unashamed of their pleasures for they were ignorant of the concept of sin. Even their temples testified to their affirmation of life, being like palaces, airy and open to the world, a place of song and dance. Worshippers chose their fattest calf for sacrifice willingly because they enjoyed the feast *with* the gods:

> Höher war der Gabe Wert gestiegen,
> Die der Geber freundlich *mit* genoss,
> Näher war der Schöpfer dem Vergnügen,
> Das im Busen des Geschöpfes floss.

> Higher valued came to be the treasure,
> Of the gift, the donor *shared* its taste,
> Stronger the creator felt the pleasure
> Which in his creature's breast did race.

Life on earth was of such quality that "Götter, die vom Himmel niederwallten, / Sahen hier ihn wieder aufgetan" ("Gods who wandered down from heaven / Saw it appear again here"). Finally, when time came for death, they were able to accept it calmly because they were reconciled to necessity.

What has replaced this vanished world, asks the poet? Cold rationality on the one hand, an impoverished vision of the divine on the other. Although he does not mention names, he refers to the Enlightenment and to certain aspects of Christianity. Rationalism is a poor way of interpreting the world because it reduces everything to a set of mathematical equations. Such a philosophy of life is soulless and inhuman. Where once poetry adorned knowledge with beauty, we now confront the bare fact, the naked truth, the rational explanation. Rosy-fingered Dawn no longer colors the morning sky, but the Earth rotates from West to East around a hot sphere of gas according to the laws of gravitation. Rationalism has cost us our intimacy with nature. It has impoverished life instead of enriching it:

Unbewusst der Freuden, die sie schenket,
Nie entzückt von ihrer Herrlichkeit,
Nie gewahr des Geistes, der sie lenket,
Sel'ger nie durch meine Seligkeit,
Fühllos selbst für ihres Künstlers Ehre,
Gleich dem toten Schlag der Pendeluhr,
Dient sie knechtisch dem Gesetz der Schwere,
Die entgötterte Natur.

Unaware of joys she is dispensing,
Never by her excellence bewitched,
Nor the hand that leads her ever sensing,
By my gratitude not once enriched,
To her artist's honor senseless even,
With the pendulum's lifeless stroke in stride,
Slave to laws of gravity, she's driven,
Nature, when de-sanctified.

Schiller reserves his severest words for Christianity's attitude toward man, life, and God. It is sad, he says, that a universe of gods, a way of life, had to perish to make way for the One: "*Einen* zu bereichern, unter allen, / Musste diese Götterwelt vergehen" ("*One* to enrich above all others, / Must a world of gods decline, disappear"). And over the desolate void broods the Word. Its essence is truth. He is a dark shadow Whom we worship in silent gloom. Abstinence and renunciation please Him: "Finster, wie er selbst, ist seine Hülle, / Mein Entsagen—was ihn feiern kann" ("Somber, like himself, is his attire, / My renouncement—all the praise he rates"). He has no friends, no brothers, no equals. Incomprehensible to the mind and unembraceable by emotion, He contemplates through the eons—himself. The poem ends with an exhortation to God either to give man the means of comprehending Him and His truth and His pleasures ("die strenge Göttin") or send him beauty ("ihre sanftere Schwester") to make all this endurable:

Dessen Strahlen mich darnieder schlagen,
Werk und Schöpfer des Verstandes! dir
Nach zu ringen, gib mir Flügel, Waagen
Dich zu wägen—oder nimm von mir
Nimm die ernste strenge Göttin wieder,
Die den Spiegel blendend vor mir hält;
Ihre sanftre Schwester sende nieder,
Spare jene für die andre Welt.

You, whose lightnings have me prostrate lying,
Work and maker of the mind, I pray,
Give me wings and courage to go vying
With you, weighing you—or take away,
Take this earnest goddess I am facing
Who for me holds up the mirror's glare,
With her gentler sister her replacing,
For the other world the former spare.

The poem tells us that Schiller's world view is similar to that of the ancient Greeks. Both rank man high in the scheme of things and both place ultimate value on existence itself. The Greek view appealed to Schiller not only because it deifies man and affirms life but, most important, because it promotes self-improvement and progress, which are the basic principles underlying his essay on aesthetics. Schiller disapproved of the Christian view because it encourages man to cultivate a low opinion of himself. In the eighteenth century some Christian sects, such as the Pietists, looked on man as an insignificant, helpless, sinful worm in a chain of being spiraling upward to the Almighty. In Schiller's view, such a notion profanes the deity, for it makes Him "nur der Würmer Erster, Edelster." ("first and noblest worm.") The Greeks saw it the other way around: "Da die Götter menschlicher waren, / Waren Menschen göttlicher" ("when the gods were more human / Human beings were more divine"). After having been exposed to this dismal picture of mankind's deplorable lot, we encounter the opposite view in *Die Künstler.*

Die Künstler (1789) is an essay in verse on the ascent of man. It begins with a eulogy to mankind's cumulative achievements. Free through reason and strong through law, master of nature and not its slave, man has reached the point where he can shape his own destiny. We can be rightfully proud of our achievements. But in our enthusiasm let us not fail to praise the artists who, through aesthetic semblance, made our ascent possible.

Before the dawn of art, Schiller tells us, man lived like a wild beast, bound by instinct and motivated by his appetites. The world appeared to him as a jumble of threatening forms. But one day, as this creature squatted by a primeval stream, he noticed a tree's reflection in the water and suddenly realized that form can be separated from matter, semblance from substance. His mimetic faculty stimulated, he traced the tree's outline in the sand. At that moment art was born. This is a revolutionary event because it launched mankind on a continuous course of development: pictorial abstraction led to abstract thinking. Thus man was able to develop his faculty for appreciating order, quality, harmony, and symmetry. Expanding the world beyond physical reality, the artists led mankind toward observation and reflection, and there arose philosophy, science, and government. In the twenty-second stanza, Schiller projects this progression toward a time in the future when man will have attained to such heights that he no longer fears death:

> Mit dem Geschick in hoher Einigkeit,
> Gelassen hingestützt auf Grazien und Musen,
> Empfängt er das Geschoss, das ihn bedräut,
> Mit freundlich dargebotnem Busen,
> Vom sanften Bogen der Notwendigkeit.

> With fate in high unity,
> Leaning calmly on Graces and Muses,
> He receives the shot that threatens him,
> His breast offered amicably,
> From the gentle bow of necessity.

Projecting his vision of man yet further, he sees art leading him to ever higher levels of aesthetic development until he achieves cosmic union with Truth:

> Zuletzt, am reifen Ziel der Zeiten,
> Noch eine glückliche Begeisterung,
> Des jüngsten Menschenalters Dichterschwung,
> Und—in der *Wahrheit* Arme wird er gleiten.

> Finally at the ripe goal of the ages,
> One more delightful enthusiasm,
> A poetic leap into the newest age of man
> And—he glides into the arms of *truth*.

Schiller concludes his poem with an appeal to the artists of the world. For if life and civilization imitate art, man's destiny is in their hands. Consequently, they should devote themselves to the creation of such art as will make further ascent possible.

Die Künstler is the last poem of Schiller's second period. When he begins writing poetry again in June 1795, he is at the height of his intellectual and artistic powers. Among the first poems of the third period are the elegies *Der Tanz* [The Dance] and *Der Spaziergang* [The Walk] both written in the summer of 1795.

In structuring our account of *Der Tanz*, we might imagine the poet-philosopher watching the courtiers and ladies of the Weimar court execute the intricacies of a formal dance. At first, he marvels at the illusion of spontaneity, freedom, and weightlessness: "Siehe, wie schwebenden Schritts im Wellenschwung sich die Paare / Drehen, den Boden berührt kaum der geflügelte Fuss" ("Look here, how swaying in step, in surging swells are the couples / Spinning! Their feet, as on wings, barely come down to the ground"). Soon the dance reminds him of the creative process. As such, it is not only pleasant to watch, but also constitutes an intellectual experience, for one can also perceive in it something about the nature of art and about the inner workings of the universe. A development in the dance evokes this insight. A couple breaks rank, turning the dance floor into confusion; or so it seems, for in reality the dancers are starting a new formation. When it is complete, the same order reconstitutes itself in a new form: "Nein, dort schwebt es frohlock-end herauf, der Knoten entwirrt sich,/Nur mit verändertem Reiz stellet die Regel sich her."

The poet has also observed that whenever the dancers make a new formation, they destroy the preceding one. Thus, destruction and creation are not polarities, but different manifestations of the creative process. There cannot be one without the other. Thus what we see on the dance floor is the universe in microcosm. Like the dance, the processes of the universe—whether destructive, constructive, or creative—are governed by law. "Ewig zerstört, es erzeugt sich ewig die drehende Schöpfung, / Und ein stilles Gesetz lenkt der Verwandlungen Spiel," ("Always destroyed, and always renewed, is the spinning creation, / By an ordinance mute the play of mutations is ruled").

Now Schiller poses a question. How is it that the forms of the dance can fluctuate ceaselessly and yet give the illusion of permanence, freedom and *Ruhe* ("tranquility")? Why is it that each dancer obeys only himself yet keeps his own appointed way through the whirling throng? It is because the dancers obey the rules:

Sprich, wie geschieht's, dass rastlos erneut die Bildungen schwanken
Und die Ruhe besteht in der bewegten Gestalt,
Jeder ein Herrscher, frei, nur dem eigenen Herzen gehorchet
Und im eilenden Lauf findet die einzige Bahn?
Willst du es wissen? Es ist Wohllauts mächtige Gottheit,
Die zum geselligen Tanz ordnet den tobenden Sprung.

Tell, how it happens, that renewed without cease the forms fluctuate
And peace prevails in moving forms,
Each one a ruler, free, of his heart's commands only mindful,
And in the hurrying dance finds the only course.
Wouldn't you like to know? It's harmony's powerful godhead
That in sociable dance orders the rampaging leap.

The poet's questions show that he is reminded most of his essay on aesthetic education, which he has just completed. *Bewegte Gestalt* ("moving form") in the question above is a synonym for *lebende Gestalt* ("living form"), his term for play and beauty in the *Fifteenth Letter*. In play opposites cooperate. The rational faculty satisfies its needs by producing forms for sensual enjoyment. Applying this principle to the dance, the *Formtrieb* produces rules and rhythms that gratify the appetites of the *Stofftrieb*. The result is that flesh and spirit, feeling and form, visible and invisible, permanence and change are fused and become indistinguishable. And again, when the poet says that it is harmony which transforms the savage's "tobenden Sprung" into dance, he recalls a remark from the *Twenty-Seventh Letter* where he says that it is through artistic forms that "der gesetzlose Sprung der Freude zum Tanz wird" ("Uncoordinated leaps of joy turn into dance"). Schiller therefore saw dance as an example of the civilizing influence of artistic play. He believed that we owe civilization to art because the more we act in accordance with aesthetic forms, the more civilized, the freer, we become. *Der Tanz* is therefore also a metaphor for civilized progress.

Suddenly, the last six lines of the poem take a new direction as the poet apparently pauses to look around at the other guests, discovering that he is the only one actually contemplating the dance. This observation engenders some cruel questions addressed to those of us who are blind to the deeper significance of things. Does the harmony of the spheres reverberate in vain for you, he asks the reader? Do you not hear it? Are you not swept up by the force of the music? Are you numb to the rhythm of life as well? The reason is: "das du im Spiele doch ehrst, fliehst du im Handeln, das Mass" ("Measure in play you respect, which in your actions you flee").

Whereas *Der Tanz* concerns the place of law in the scheme of things, *Der Spaziergang* expounds the development of civilization in general. It emphasizes the necessity of a harmonious relationship between man and nature. The narrator of this poem decides to take a long walk. Following a road that eventually ascends a mountain, he has a panoramic view of the plains below, upon which he perceives the history of civilization. In one part he sees pristine nature, in another cultivated fields, then villages, and further on the horizon the skyline of a great city. Each signifies a stage in cultural evolution: savage innocence, the invention of agriculture, and the rise of urban life. He observes that in the villages nature is the companion of man. But the cities subjugate nature to create civilized life. As civilization develops, religion and law are introduced. Private property and free enterprise begin to thrive. Trade develops which brings men into contact with other civilizations. The arts flourish, and philosophers ponder the human condition. Finally comes the invention of printing, which ranks high among man's achievements: "durch der Jahrhunderte Strom trägt ihn das redende Blatt" ("Now the talking leaves carry him along the stream of centuries"). Knowledge vanquishes ignorance. Man seeks the truth, and the truth sets him free.

At some point in its upward course, a civilization may commit a fatal error and cause its own destruction. Not content to be the master of nature, man wants to dispense with it altogether. Then comes chaos:

> Freiheit ruft die Vernunft, Freiheit die wilde Begierde,
>   Von der heil'gen Natur ringen sie lüstern sich los.
> Ach, da reissen im Sturm die Anker, die an dem Ufer
>   Warnend ihn hielten, ihn fasst mächtig der flutende Strom,
> Ins Unendliche reisst er ihn hin, die Küste verschwindet.

> Freedom, cries our reason, freedom, cry the wild desires,
>   Both of them greedily break nature's holy embrace.
> Ah, the anchors break in the storm, which as a warning
> Tied him close to the coast, mighty torrential tides
> Pull him into the infinite flood, and gone is the coastline.

Deprived of nature's guiding principle, man loses his orientation and his roots. He is like the man in a boat swept out to sea with neither sail nor paddle. Values are turned upside down. Mendacity, hypocrisy, greed, blasphemy, and artificiality win the victory over honesty and fair play. Social ties dissolve. Eventually, the whole edifice collapses in revolution. Schiller here has his own age in mind. As a solution to the problem he proposed that man relearn to live in harmony with nature.

One of the first things we notice when we examine *Der Spazier-*

gang closely is its cyclical structure. The poem begins and ends with nature. The development of thought, however, is linear. Man does not return to his savage beginnings. Rather he rejoins nature in an improved relationship in the future. Thus Schiller's thinking is based on the principle of improvement: In the beginning, man is guided by instinct like all other creatures. Eventually, he emerges from blind submission to where nature is his companion. Up to this point, each stage is better than the last. Man begins to undermine this process when he tries to do without nature altogether. Freedom is a dangerous and treacherous force. Like a sword that cuts both ways, it makes progress possible but it destroys when unchecked by the rightful claims of nature. No human path leads out of the predicament. Only nature, which is independent of the human condition, offers a solution. Like nature, we must learn to renew ourselves in a continuous cycle of spiritual rebirths.

The theme of progress through acting in accordance with law reappears in some of the ballads, a genre in which Schiller excelled. When he wrote his first ballad in 1797, he was an experienced author of wide knowledge. His subjects range from classical antiquity through history to legends and myths. In choosing a story, Schiller was concerned equally with its lyrical potential and its suitability for expressing the ideal. A survey of underlying ideas provides an impression of the scope of his ballads. The theme of *Der Ring des Polycrates* dramatizes the Greek view of Providence as a force that gives before taking away. In *Die Kraniche des Ibykus* art avenges a murder. In *Der Gang nach dem Eisenhammer* deception destroys the deceiver. *Das Eleusische Fest* describes humanity's rise from barbarism. The subject of *Die Bürgschaft* is true friendship, that of *Der Kampf mit dem Drachen* shows when one principle takes precedence over another.

Among Schiller's most enduring ballads is *Das Lied von der Glocke* [The Song of the Bell] written in 1799. Many of its lines have become proverbial. Until recently, it numbered among the poems that German school children memorized. Even the man in the street knows a line or two. Among the reasons for the wide appeal of Schiller's ballads, careful preparation ranks near the top. In gathering material for this piece, Schiller visited a foundry where he studied each stage in the casting of a bell. The process furnishes the ballad's structural principle: To cast a bell melt copper and tin, add potash, heat the mixture at just the right temperature, then pour it into a clay mold buried in the ground. After it hardens, lift it out, smash the mold, and the bell hangs free. The action of the poem begins the day the bell is cast.

The master bell maker, who narrates the story, instructs the apprentices as to the deeper significance of creating a bell. Man, he says, should always reflect upon his actions because this distinguishes him from the other creatures. So he uses the casting as an extended metaphor for the human condition and civilization. His underlying purpose is to affirm certain values.

The master observes that we apply the same values to bell making that we esteem in daily life. Purity, for instance, commands our admiration. As we skim the foam to purify the metal, so we honor the purity of the newborn child whose birth the bell proclaims. When the child grows up, he too will break the childhood mold and go out into the world to seek his fortune. As potash promotes fusion, so experience fuses the character. At last, he returns home and falls madly in love with the girl he left behind. The mixing of elements to form a prized alloy is also like marriage, where the strong and the weak combine to make a better third:

> Denn wo das Strenge mit dem Zarten,
> Wo Starkes sich und Mildes paarten,
> Da gibt es einen guten Klang

> Wherever strictness with the tender,
> Where the strong and the soft combine,
> The sound they make is clear and fine.

Therefore, let those who are in love be sure that they mix well so that firm ground remains after marriage cures the temporary insanity. The poet goes afield to describe the ideal home complete with bustling housewife and agreeable aromas.

In the thirteenth stanza the master pours the liquid metal into the mold buried in the ground. The casting complete, he proclaims a day of rest while it hardens. In the following stanzas, he digresses to enlarge upon the benefits of civilization, the greatest of which is peace which, in turn, is based upon law and order. Technology, science, agriculture, and the arts are all founded upon order:

> Heil'ge Ordnung, segenreiche
> Himmelstochter, die das Gleiche
> Frei und leicht und freudig bindet,
> Die der Städte Bau gegründet,

Die herein von den Gefilden
Rief den ungesell'gen Wilden,
Eintrat in der Menschen Hütte,
Sie gewöhnt zu sanften Sitten
Und das teuerste der Bande
Wob, den Trieb zum Vaterlande!

Holy order, bounties spreading,
Heaven's daughter, equals wedding
In a free and willing union,
Bonding force of town communion,
From the fields who called the rustic
And the savage turned domestic,
Huts of humans penetrated,
Gentle customs inculcated,
Forged, moved by sublime desire,
Bonds of patriotic fire.

In the twenty-second stanza the master shatters the mold. Here occurs the famous line: "Wenn die Glock soll auferstehen, / Muss die Form in Stücken gehen" ("For the bell is born unfettered / Only when the mold is shattered"). In other words, destruction precedes creation, death rebirth. Yet no matter how careful we are in our endeavors, misfortune lurks nearby. Suppose the cauldron cracks and torrents of molten metal rush out and incinerate us all. The same happens in life when the mold of the law breaks and wild emotion spills out, such as in the French Revolution, where a crazed throng dictated the course of events.

Fortunately, the mold holds and the casting has been a success. In the last stanza the bell hangs free, glistening in the sun. The craftsmen gather around to christen it *Concordia*. The final words are "*Friede* sei ihr erst Geläute" ("let *peace* be its first sound").

Despite this ballad's enduring popularity, its appeal is not universal. Many regard its values as hopelessly bourgeois and threadbare. Granted, reading the poem may seem similar to turning the pages in a collection of Currier and Ives prints. The homespun verities seem trite to us: the bustling housewife taking care of the children, the breadwinner proudly watching his family grow, early to bed and early to rise, along with moderation and simplicity in all endeavor are values that have little to say to a world poised at the threshold of nuclear oblivion. If the piece had nothing else to offer, we might declare it irrelevant. In order to appreciate it, we must look beyond its oaken bucket, motherhood-and-apple-pie images.

In the first place, the poem is more than a story about a bell casting ornamented with sage pronouncements. It describes a creative act exemplifying Schiller's theory of art. We have learned that art produces things for both intellectual and sensual pleasure. By teaching us new ways to perceive, art multiplies enjoyment. We see the bell and appreciate its form and color. We feel it and enjoy the texture, we hear it and take pleasure in the musical sound. Enjoyment therefore resides both in the process and in the product. Schiller is saying that we should cultivate our capacity for appreciating art. The prerequisite for such aesthetic education is social stability, which brings up the next point.

When Schiller wrote this ballad, it appeared as if the French Revolution might spill across the Rhine at any moment. Many Germans hoped that it would and dedicated themselves to that end. The prospect of a German Revolution frightened Schiller, who knew that his country could not avoid the chaos any better than the French. So he portrayed the upheaval negatively, which accords with his ideas about social evolution. As he points out not only in the ballad but also in the *Fourth Letter*, true improvement in human rights depend on a citizenry properly prepared for it by education. If the government grants freedoms without first educating the citizens to it, chaos results. Schiller saw his ideas confirmed in the Reign of Terror and in the Prison Massacres of 1792. The madness and the butchery proved to him that the French had moved too fast. The Revolution failed because the average citizen could neither understand, nor cope with, the new moral principles. Education relying on art is the key to progress. It presupposes stability, because a hungry and frightened man has no time for learning. Like the clay mold of the bell, law and order shape man and contain his destructive impulses.

Throughout the ballad, the bell serves a metaphor for unity and harmony. The poet compares it to the institutions of marriage, the family, friendship, and society, which are also composed of different elements. Or again, as the cooperation of the craftsmen produces a bell, so the unified efforts of the citizenry create a better society. Finally, the tolling bell unifies the community in musical sound.

The theme of harmony, along with its manifestation as play, ranks among Schiller's favorite subjects. It turns up again in the ballads *Der Taucher* [The Diver] and *Der Handschuh* [The Glove].

In *Der Taucher*, the king and his court are assembled by the Straits of Messina at the precipice overlooking Charybdis, an ocean whirlpool infamous ever since Odysseus nearly drowned there The waters boil, hiss, crash, and roar. Objects caught in its pull are sucked down, wasted across the rocks, and belched forth in fragments. Into this howling place the king casts a golden goblet. Then he says to the knights and squires assembled around him that if anyone is brave enough to go after it, he can keep it as a royal gift. Three times the king speaks, but none of the men step forward. Suddenly a young squire strides to the edge of the precipice and plunges right down into the funnel. Four suspenseful stanzas later he emerges holding the goblet. The court throngs to shout his praise. The princess fills the goblet with wine. The youth tells of another, fantastic realm of strange sights and stranger creatures. He reports that he discovered the goblet lodged in some coral overhanging an endless abyss filled with purple darkness and gliding shadows. He seized the goblet just as something started toward him. At that moment, the force of the current swept him back to the surface. Never again, he concludes, would he descend into that place of fear. Fascinated, the king compliments the daring exploit and proposes another dive. If the squire will bring back descriptions of the purple unknown that glooms beyond the coral, he will have a fabulous ring for reward. The princess, who likes the youth, intervenes:

> "Lass Vater genug sein das grausame Spiel!
> Er hat Euch bestanden, was keiner besteht,
> Und könnt Ihr des Herzens Gelüsten nicht zähmen,
> So mögen die Ritter den Knappen beschämen."

> "Don't, father, enough of this gruesome game!
> For you he's accomplished, what others did not,
> If nothing can still the thirst of your desire,
> So let the knights shame the Squire."

The king responds by hurling the goblet into the abyss with the promise that he will include his daughter into the bargain. The squire looks at the princess. His eyes gleam. He dives and never returns.

As far as its meaning is concerned, the ballad is primarily a scathing indictment of irresponsible rulers. A brave and talented youth must perish because his highness likes exciting games. Nothing matters as long as his majesty enjoys himself. When the squire returns to tell his tale, the king is delighted, not so much at his safe return but because the game can go on. The fun is not over.

Now he can propose an expedition into the deep purple. He is happier still when his daughter displays affection for the squire, for now he can offer her as the grand prize and so add tender emotion to the game. He is completely absorbed in the thrill of the wager. His behavior reduces the two young people to mere instruments of his pleasure. Still, the king does not bear full responsibility for what happens. The squire is not under orders to return to the abyss. He can refuse. He chooses to play the game because he wants the prize, which brings up the next point.

The youth perishes because he violates a primary principle of conduct advanced by Schiller who, in his essay on aesthetics, asserts that men who live life as an end in itself, men who play, will fare better than those who live for gain. Both ways of life are illustrated in *Der Taucher*. In the first part of the ballad, the squire displays no interest in the goblet as such. For him, it is an object to prove where he has been. He makes the first dive following a spontaneous impulse to indulge his talent. It is a process-oriented act and therefore qualifies as play. The second time, however, he dives for gain. Now he becomes goal-oriented. Play becomes work. At that moment, he joins the multitude for whom "der Genuss wurde von der Arbeit, das Mittel vom Zweck, die Anstrengung von der Belohnung geschieden" ("enjoyment is divorced from labor, the means from the end, the effort from the reward," VI, 7).

What happens to the squire reflects society's goals in the formation of its members. In its early years we encourage the child to play, to enjoy games and activity for the sake of the pleasure involved. Then, at some point, we tell him that it is time to stop playing and grow up. Activity must be turned to practical account. Be goal-oriented, we advise, because happiness lies in the reward. This endless, revolving wheel of desire and gratification is like the maelstrom of the ballad which spins its victims down to moral degradation.

Fortunately, there are heroes like Delorges of *Der Handschuh* who are not for sale at any price.

In a letter to Goethe dated 18 June 1797 Schiller called *Der Handschuh* a little postscript to *Der Taucher*. The two ballads are similar but end differently. In both, the hero becomes the object of someone's whim and in both he tempts death. Unlike the hero of *Der Taucher*, who risks his life for reward and perishes, Delorges risks his life for no motive of gain and survives. And he returns to punish the affront.

Unlike the tone of *Der Taucher,* that of *Der Handschuh* is lighthearted and gay. The piece begins with the royal court in full regalia seated around an arena in hopes of excitement. A hatch opens and Schiller's favorite animal, the lion, enters majestically. Next comes a tiger, followed by two leopards who pounce upon him with savage fury. With a royal roar the King of Beasts quells the brawl. The cats settle down in wary coexistence. Suddenly, Lady Kunigunde drops her glove right down between the lion and the tiger. Turning to the knight Delorges, she says with a mock:

> Herr Ritter, ist Eure Lieb' so heiss,
> Wie Ihr mir's schwört zu jeder Stund,
> Ei, so hebt mir den Handschuh auf.

> Sir Knight, if your love's so hot,
> As you're swearing all the time,
> Well, go pick up my glove for me.

Delorges quickly descends into the arena, picks up the glove, and returns. The court shouts his praise. But Lady Kunigunde receives him "mit zärtlichem Liebesblick— / Er verheisst ihm sein nahes Glück" ("with tender looks of lust— / Which promise forthcoming delight"). Delorges, however, hurls the glove into her face with the words "Den Dank Dame, begehr' ich nicht,"/ Und verlässt sie zur selben Stunde" ("I don't want thanks, lady, / And walks out on her the same minute").

In considering the meaning of the ballad, we observe that Lady Kunigunde resembles the king of *Der Taucher* as a representative of egotism and moral turpitude. She has known all along that Delorges loves her, but she is insensitive. For if she had any feelings at all for him, she would have called him back with anxious words because she could not endure the sight of his mangled body. As far as she is concerned, though, he is simply an object for her amusement. So she puts him to the test, dropping her glove into the arena as if she were playing fetch-the-stick with her dog; and she intends to reward him like one by allowing him to worship in her bedchamber.

Delorges perceives her moral corruption in a sudden realization when he sees the expression "which promises forthcoming delight." It means that she thinks he risked his life for the reward. She does not understand that he retrieved the glove in a spontaneous impulse to indulge his courage—like the squire—and to express his feeling for her. She does not comprehend that reward corrupts not only the integrity of his deed as a playful, process-oriented act but that it also trivializes his love. His response is just what Schiller means by naive behavior provoked by the unexpected. Delorges's deed is a reflex moral action emanating from nobility of character. Consequently, his reaction and Kunigunde's humiliation please the reader because—as we recall from Schiller's essay on poetry—whenever we see the genuine and the false side by side, and when we witness the former unmasking the latter, and when we know that right prevails, we experience moral pleasure. The feeling that justice prevails also attends *Das Verschleierte Bild zu Sais* [The Veiled Statue of Sais].

The story is about a student who in searching for truth breaks a law and discovers guilty conscience. At the beginning of the ballad we learn that he has come to Sais in ancient Egypt in the pursuit of truth. But after several months of hard work he has made little headway. He complains to his teachers that they have not revealed the truth to him, and that he is no nearer his goal now than when he started. Is not truth an indivisible totality which can be shown to him, he asks? Yet here it is handled like something which one possesses in degree "wie der Sinne Glück" ("like sensual pleasure"). Learning is useless, he proclaims, if the parts conceal the whole: "Was hab' ich, / Wenn ich nicht alles habe?" ("What have I, / If I haven't got everything?"). At Sais one does not see the forest for the trees.

Speaking of these things with his master, the student notices a huge statue of the veiled goddess Isis. What is behind the veil, he asks? Truth, responds the master, but to lift the veil is forbidden to mortal man; only the goddess herself may lift it. If a person looks anyway, "der *sieht* die Wahrheit" ("he *sees* truth"). The student is tempted and the master warns him of dire consequences; for though the veil is light to the touch, breaking the law weighs heavy on the conscience.

That night the student cannot sleep. Aflame with curiosity he tosses and turns. At midnight he rises, shyly makes his way to the deserted temple, jumps over the wall, and approaches the statue. Disregarding an inner voice that warns him, he uncovers the face. Next morning the priests find him senseless at the base of the statue. From that day onward he lives a joyless life, and he dies a welcome, early death from remorse. He never tells what he saw, but when pressed he would say: "Weh dem, der zu der Wahrheit geht durch Schuld, / Sie wird ihm nimmermehr erfreulich sein" ("Woe be unto him who goes to truth through guilt / He will never enjoy it").

Among other things this ballad is about the nature of truth. Since its appreciation is enhanced by some acquaintance with truth theories, a discussion is called for. In broad terms, Schiller's conception of truth shares the characteristics of the coherence theory of truth propounded by the system-building philosophers Leibniz, Spinoza, Kant, Hegel, and F.H. Bradley. According to this theory, truth is not a single whole but a vast system of logically interrelated propositions—just as the elements of pure mathematics are interrelated. This body of propositions is useful in organizing the flux of experience into meaning. To verify the truth of a proposition is to determine if it coheres with a system of related propositions, and if it is logically deducible from them. In short, the better our principles cohere with the system, the truer they are.

Schiller was particularly interested in the way truthful propositions are manufactured. In the *Twenty-Third Letter* we read that truth is a modulation of the aesthetic condition and that it is man-made. Truth "ist etwas, das die Denkkraft selbsttätig und in ihrer Freiheit hervorbringt" ("is something produced by our thinking faculty, autonomously and by virtue of its freedom"). We should think of Schiller's truth as an automatic operation of the mind in which we either realize or create propositions that cohere with the system. Now we understand why in the ballad Schiller depicts truth as a goddess whose veil only she herself may lift: truth reveals itself when we are ready for it; we do not seek it so much as it seeks us.

The student, on the other hand, holds the popular belief that truth is a single whole, a timeless archetype: "Ist sie nicht eine einzige, ungeteilte?" ("is it not a single, indivisible One?"). Unable to produce truth from within, he seeks it in the outside world. And he believes that he is capable of understanding the truth not only about nature but also about the nature of man. Schiller attacks this conception again in his essay *Über das Erhabene,* pointing out that if we define truth as the one principle to which all others relate, or as an account of the world in its totality, this truth would be beyond comprehension because it transcends finite experience. We should concern ourselves only with what is thinkable by man. Schiller's truth is personal, dynamic, and progressive—not eternal or absolute. We do indeed possess it in degree. Since the mind can produce truthful propositions only from the aesthetic condition, we have one more reason to strive for it.

The ballad ends ironically. In pursuing truth as a physical object, the student demonstrates how the proposition "if we incur guilt in reaching our goals, we will not enjoy them" coheres with such others as "the end does not justify the means," or as Faust discovers, the process is more important than the goal.

Following the ballads, Schiller wrote several poems which he categorized as *Lieder* ("songs"), a verse form peculiar to Germany. The requirements are that the piece express emotions in a straight-forward way, literally not figuratively. The structure is simple; the *Lied* is usually divided into stanzas, and it employs rhyme. There are no restrictions on subject matter or on the feelings represented. Accordingly, Schiller's *Lieder* are free of abstract thought and display the strictest simplicity in form and language. They are the most lyrical of his achievements. The elegiac tone characterizes most of them, as they express sadness at lost joy, at a golden age now vanished, or with the ideal unattained. Representative of this genre are *Sehnsucht* [Longing] written in 1801 and *Der Pilgrim* [The Pilgrim] composed in 1803.

Sehnsucht is about an unhappy man dwelling in a dreary valley enshrouded by cold fog. He is dissatisfied with his lot and thirsts to live in a tropical wonderland nearby. His discomfort is particularly acute whenever the wind brings melodious sounds and agreeable aromas from there. Through dark foliage he spies the glow of golden fruit. His longing carries him away when he imagines himself a resident of that place:

> Ach, wie schön muss sich's ergehen
> Dort im ewigen Sonnenschein,
> Und die Luft auf jene Höhen,
> O wie labend muss sie sein!

> Oh, how great in the eternal
> Sunshine things must be up there,
> On those hills, forever vernal,
> Soothing there must be the air!

Getting to the wonderland, however, is no easy matter, for in between rages a river which fills him with fear. But one day he sees a boat tossing near the shore. It is without a helmsman, yet he decides to take it anyway because:

> Du musst glauben, du musst wagen,
> Denn die Götter leihn kein Pfand,
> Nur ein Wunder kann dich tragen
> In das schöne Wunderland.

You have to believe you have to dare
Since the deities give no pawn
Only a wonder can pay your fare
To the lovely wonderland.

The subject of the poem is man's longing for the ideal. The man living in the valley of the cloud represents man in his limited actuality; the distant wonderland with its harmonies, aromas, and symbolical fruit signifies the ideal. His yearning is the poetic representation of man's longing for a better place. The raging current stands for the dangers inherent in striving. Unfortunately, there are no signposts to help us along the way or guides to lead us. Nor should we expect the gods to carry us across miraculously. We must make the journey alone. We must face down our fears and take the chance.

In good poetry sound and meaning go hand in hand. Schiller's skill in marrying sound to sense is particularly evident in *Sehnsucht*. Take the first octave, for example:

Ach, aus dieses Tales Gründen,
Die der kalte Nebel drückt,
Könnt' ich doch den Ausgang finden.
Ach wie fühlt' ich mich beglückt!
Dort erblick' ich schöne Hügel,
Ewig jung und ewig grün!
Hätt' ich Schwingen, hätt' ich Flügel,
Nach den Hügeln zög' ich hin.

From this valley's deep abysses,
By a frigid fog oppressed,
Could I flee its precipices,
Oh, what joy would fill my breast!
Lovely hills I'd be discerning,
Ageless, greening without care,
Had I pinions, wings, my yearning
Would suffice to take me there.

The subject of the first four lines is the narrator's misery and longing. Immediately, the onomatopoeic words "ach, aus" create an auditory image of pain and sighing. Since the caesura falls between them they become spondees, the most unrhythmical of meters reflecting the most unharmonious of lives. To further convey the sense of malaise by sound, Schiller makes the first lines hard to pronounce. By alternating light and dark vowels, and by choosing words in which the majority of accented syllables begin and end with a strong consonant or group of consonants which do not flow together (es-Gr; el-dr) he forces the reader to reshape his mouth between syllables. As the syllables collide the tempo slows and the rhythmical quality suffers—like the man. By contrast, the lines describing the wonderland are remarkably smooth. The rhythm is swift and regular. The words end in vowels or in consonants that are easily run together and fairly glide off the tongue, thus conveying the perfection of the ideal.

Similar to *Sehnsucht* in form and content is *Der Pilgrim*. In a way it is a continuation of the former, since it describes the quester's actual labors and their outcome. In the *Lied,* the poet sees himself as a pilgrim who never reaches his goal. His story is brief. When still a youth, he left the comforts of home and family and with a light heart embarked upon a pilgrimage. Sustained by faith and powerful hopes, he looks for the golden gate where the transitory turns eternal:

> Bis zu einer goldnen Pforten
> Du gelangst, da gehst du ein,
> Denn das Irdische wird dorten
> Himmlisch unvergänglich sein.

> To a golden gate to wander
> Was my goal, to go inside,
> For all earthly things up yonder
> Heavenly unchanged abide.

Day and night he sought, never resting, never finding. Mountain heights he conquered, and forded torrents. He surmounted every obstacle. Hopefully choosing a river flowing East, he enters a large ocean. Now infinite emptiness is all around. He is no nearer his goal than before. Heaven and earth will never unite, he agonizes, and "there" is never "here."

> Ach kein Steg will dahin führen,
> Ach der Himmel über mir
> Will die Erde nie berühren,
> Und das Dort ist niemals hier!

> No paths run in that direction,
> Overhead, blue heaven's sphere
> Never makes with earth connection,
> And the There is never Here!

Unlike *Sehnsucht*, which ends optimistically, *Der Pilgrim* despairs that he is no nearer his goal. The *Lied* concludes pessimistically. Even so, the pilgrim never doubts the existence of the ideal, which is Schiller's way of saying that we can have the ideal in the Here and Now. Thus Schiller does not conceive of eternity as another dimension where we go when we die; rather, in his view, we turn the transitory into the eternal here and know heaven on Earth.

Finally, there is a need for discussing the pieces as examples of the elegiac mode. In his essay on poetry, Schiller explains that the elegy expresses sadness at something lost. The emotion of sadness is evoked only by the idea of what is lost, not by the thing itself. Because modern man is divided between feeling and reason, he must first filter his impressions through an idea before he can feel. Consequently, the poet evokes the proper emotions not by describing the wonderland and the golden gate as actual places, but by making them metaphors for the desire of us all to live at peace and in harmony with ourselves and with our environment. Our sadness, therefore, derives from enthusiasm awakened by the ideal.

Most of the poems discussed so far are written in falling meter. Trochaic and dactylic feet are more suitable to the elegiac mood, Schiller's favorite, because a stressed syllable followed by an unstressed one moves downward from the emphasis—down from the golden age to the imperfect present. *Das Mädchen aus der Fremde* [The Maiden from Far Away], written in 1796, belongs to a minority of poems composed in rising meter. The iambic foot moves upward to the emphasis and so enhances the optimistic flavor. *Das Mädchen aus der Fremde* is also free of abstract thought. It is pure poetic fantasy where the value resides in the imagery and in the excellence of expression. The poem is short enough to quote it all as an example of Schiller's lyrical powers at their best.

> In einem Tal bei armen Hirten
> Erschien mit jedem jungen Jahr,
> Sobald die ersten Lerchen schwirrten,
> Ein Mädchen, schön und wunderbar.

Sie war nicht in dem Tal geboren,
Man wusste nicht, woher sie kam,
Und schnell war ihre Spur verloren,
Sobald das Mädchen Abschied nahm.

Beseligend war ihre Nähe,
Und alle Herzen wurden weit,
Doch eine Würde, eine Höhe
Entfernte die Vertraulichkeit.

Sie brachte Blumen mit und Früchte,
Gereift auf einer andern Flur,
In einem andern Sonnenlichte,
In einer glücklichern Natur.

Und teilte jedem eine Gabe,
Dem Früchte, jenem Blumen aus,
Der Jüngling und der Greis am Stabe,
Ein jeder ging beschenkt nach Haus.

Willkommen waren alle Gäste,
Doch nahte sich ein liebend Paar,
Dem reichte sie der Gaben beste,   ˙
Der Blumen allerschönste dar.

Amidst poor shepherds, in a valley,
With every fresh and youthful year,
When dashing larks start first to rally,
A charming maiden would appear.

Who knows where she originated,
Her place of birth was not the vale,
And once she left, obliterated,
All trace of her would quickly pale.

All hearts with bliss she sent expanding,
When near, sweet joy held always sway,
But dignity, respect commanding,
All intimacy held at bay.

Along she came with fruits and flowers,
Matured upon another field,
In sunshine differing from ours,
And of a happier nature yield.

> To each a gift she had allotted,
> One, fruits, the other, flowers got,
> The young and those by old age knotted,
> Home each of them some bounty brought.
>
> A welcome to all her guests she tendered,
> But when approached a loving pair,
> Her finest gifts to them surrendered,
> Fair flowers gave beyond compare.

Various interpretations have been proposed. Some see the maiden as an allegory of poetry, the shepherds signifying man, and the valley standing for earth. Others say that since she comes in spring and is associated with fruit and flowers, she is Demeter. In my view she personifies Schiller's conception of the ideal person or of ideal beauty. The third quatrain, for instance, describes ideal beauty's effect on the beholder. In the *Fifteenth Letter* Schiller tells us that since beauty is a combination of mind and feeling, it affects the beholder in two ways at once. He illustrates what he means with a description of his reaction to the statue *Juno Ludovisi:* "Es ist weder Anmut, noch ist es Würde, was aus dem herrlichen Antlitz einer Juno Ludovisi zu uns spricht; es ist keines von beiden, weil es beides zugleich ist. Indem der weibliche Gott unsre Anbetung heischt, entzündet das gottgleiche Weib unsre Liebe" ("It is not Grace, nor is it yet Dignity, which speaks to us from the superb countenance of a Juno Ludovisi; it is neither the one nor the other because it is both at once. While the goddess demands our veneration, the god-like woman kindles our love"). This explains why the maiden from afar attracts and repels at the same time. This interpretation is reinforced by the fourth quatrain which contains Schiller's poetic metaphors for the ideal: fruit, sunlight, happier nature. This is admittedly straining after lofty significance where there may be none. In any case, the poem can be read and enjoyed for its lyrical qualities.

This concludes the chapter on poetry. It provides an overall impression of his career as a poet from early precocity to composed genius. We have seen how his style evolves from rhetorical embellishment to a classical simplicity outstanding for its musical qualities. We have studied how his lyrics evince the harmonious fusion of art and ideas, imagination and speculation, sound and sense. As the following chapters reveal, Schiller the dramatist undergoes a transfiguration similar to Schiller the poet.

CHAPTER 3

Drama of the Early and Middle Period

SCHILLER'S dramatic activity is ordinarily divided into an early, a middle, and a classical period. The drama of his youth includes *Die Räuber, Fiesko,* and *Kabale und Liebe.* These early efforts display the fiery emotionalism characteristic of the *Storm and Stress. Don Carlos* is the only play of the middle period. Reflecting his interest in high tragedy, its language is more elevated and the action more restrained. After the success of *Don Carlos,* Schiller became involved with other things. During the next ten years he studied history, assimilated Kant, and wrote his essays on aesthetics. Finally in 1797 he returned to the theater with *Wallenstein,* which marks the beginning of his classical period.

This chapter considers the drama of his early and middle period in chronological order. The discussion of each play follows the same structure. First, there is a brief account of the genesis of the piece; then a summary of the elements of the plot; and last, an analysis of the work.

I   Die Räuber

Schiller began his first drama when he was eighteen and still a medical student at Duke Karl Eugen's military academy. Until he graduated, he worked on the manuscript whenever the mood struck him and his studies allowed him the time. After his appointment as regimental surgeon in 1781, he finally found the time to complete it. Because of the play's provocative nature, he was unable to find a publisher. Not to be discouraged, he borrowed the money for a private printing and published it anonymously. Shortly after the play appeared, Dalberg—the director of the Mannheim theater—offered not only to produce the play but also any Schiller might write in the future.

Following extensive revisions for the stage, *Die Räuber* played to a full house at Mannheim on 13 January 1782. Schiller left his

70

regiment without leave to attend the first performance. *Die Räuber* stunned the audience. An eyewitness reports that the theater turned into a madhouse: some spectators stomped their feet, others shouted and screamed; strangers sobbed and embraced one another; women fainted; and so on. After Mannheim, the drama played successfully all over Germany. In 1782 alone it appeared in Hamburg, Leipzig, and Frankfurt. Berlin and Mainz followed in 1783. In 1792 at the height of the French Revolution it even played in Paris. The first performance in America took place in New York as early as 1795. Much of the drama's appeal resides in its exciting story.

A   The Elements of the Plot

Die Räuber is the story of two brothers, Karl and Franz von Moor. Since Karl is the elder, he will inherit the title. Tall, fair, and handsome, he is everybody's favorite. At school he stands out as a natural leader of men. Magnetic, strong of character, and idealistic, he is the kind of person who commands admiration. Karl loves his beautiful cousin Amalia von Edelreich, who lives at Moor Castle while Karl is away at the University of Leipzig. They plan to marry after his return.

Franz, on the other hand, is Karl's opposite in every respect. Misshapen, he is ugly to the point of revulsion. A villain of the blackest heart, resentful, malicious, and consumed by jealous hatred for Karl, he plots his demise. He begins by maligning Karl in the eyes of the count, who is old, weak, and unsuspecting. The treacherous brother composes false letters originating from a fictitious informer in Leipzig which portray Karl as a worthless profligate. He reads them aloud to the count and succeeds in getting his permission to send a mild letter of disapproval in the count's name. Exploiting the situation, he writes that their father, shocked at Karl's behavior, disowns him.

The letter reaches Karl in Leipzig at the worst possible moment (I, 6). He has been reading about great men in Plutarch's Lives and realizes how shabby his contemporaries look in comparison. Nowadays, he pronounces wrathfully, the only value is the ruthless pursuit of self-interest, and in the place of integrity and fair play we have a philosophy that says: Do it unto your neighbor before he does it unto you. The rich get richer and the poor poorer. When Franz's letter arrives, Karl has worked himself into a frenzy. The letter's petty moralizing and underlying spite disturb him deeply. He regards it as a perfect example of everything that is wrong with modern society. His father has proved to be like everyone else. When he discovers that some of his comrades plan to live as robbers, he decides on the spur of the moment to join them as their captain. Karl's attitude toward his future life reminds us in some ways of Don Quixote who, inspired by lofty but impractical ideals, sets out to defend the oppressed and to right wrongs. Accordingly, the robber chieftain does not think of himself as a criminal but as a divine messenger of retribution who appears, deus ex machina, to dispense justice. He breaks the law, he says, to enforce the spirit of the law. The authorities, on the other hand, regard the robbers as a band of bloodthirsty terrorists who rape, plunder, and kill for sport. Karl is wanted dead or alive.

Karl's greatest exploit comes when he rescues his best friend Roller from the gallows. Many townspeople are killed. Troops are called out to hunt the robbers down. Once they are surrounded, the government sends an emissary, who offers everyone in the band a royal pardon if they will but hand over their captain. The men refuse indignantly, and the battle begins. Under Karl's inspired leadership they win the day. When they are safe, Karl renews his oath never to abandon his men (III, 2).

Meanwhile, back at Moor Castle, Franz continues to spin his villainous intrigues. With Karl out of the way, he now plots his father's death. He considers various plans, finally settling on psychological warfare. He concocts an elaborate story about how Karl, despairing at his father's rejection, sought a hero's death in battle. The subterfuge calls for the old man to hold himself responsible and so die an early death from regret. Franz bribes an ambitious weakling called Hermann to dress up like a soldier and deliver to the count a heartrending account of Karl's last days and dying words. The count faints when he hears the news. When he awakens, Franz accuses him of wanting to live forever and locks him up in an abandoned tower with the intention of starving him to death. But Hermann, stricken with conscience, secretly brings him food.

In the next scene the action switches back to the robbers, presently operating out of the Bohemian Forest. Karl is dissatisfied now with every aspect of his new life. He had not expected so much savagery and senseless killing. He accuses himself, and his conscience aches. At the end of the third act, unhappy and disenchanted, he decides to return home incognito. He is welcomed into Moor Castle unrecognized in his disguise as a count upon his travels. He learns that his father is dead and that Franz is master. There are some painful scenes with Amalia, who believes that her lover is still alive. The faithful old servant Daniel recognizes Karl by a scar and urges him to leave, for Franz intends to murder him.

Arriving back at camp, Karl discovers that his men have found his father imprisoned in a tower and nearly dead. The old man does not recognize his son. Asking questions, Karl learns the extent of Franz's crimes. Determined to punish his brother, he picks an elite raiding party with the idealistic Schweitzer as its leader. Schweitzer swears to return with Franz alive or not at all. But during the attack Franz commits suicide. Unable to fulfill his oath, Schweitzer kills himself. While the men are away on the mission, Karl discovers that his father is innocent of disowning him. He joyfully reveals his identity in hopes of a reconciliation. But the shock of seeing his son's wasted life kills the old man. Just then the raiding party returns to camp. In their ignorance of circumstances they have brought Amalia with them as booty.

Amalia recognizes Karl without his disguise. For a few minutes it appears as if he will get the happiness he longs for, because Amalia loves him and forgives him. He will give up this life, marry her, and they will live in another country. Growing rebellious, the men will not allow him to leave. They remind him of the great battle when they rejected the offer of pardon and of his oath never to abandon them. Now they are ready to collect. Karl will continue on as captain, and, as a token of his integrity, Amalia is to be handed over for their amusement. When Amalia realizes that she and Karl cannot marry, she begs the robbers to kill her. As some prepare to do so, Karl shoots her himself. Then he turns to his men and tells them the sacrifice of this innocent life releases him from his oath and from any other claims they have upon him. Furthermore, he knows now that his rebellion was an ill-begotten delusion that caused more misery than it cured. He now understands the absurdity of breaking the law to uphold the law.

The drama ends with Karl planning his surrender to the authorities. To prevent this voluntary action from appearing as a deliberate effort to ameliorate his sentence, he will arrange for an impoverished day laborer with a large family to turn him in for the reward.

B   *The Ideal and Reality*

The reason why Karl meets a tragic end is because he acts out of harmony with his true nature. Though he tries to convince himself otherwise, he is neither a revolutionary nor a social reformer, and certainly not a terrorist. His true disposition is apparent at the beginning of the play when he looks forward to going home. He speaks of his father and of his future enthusiastically. Before reading his brother's letter, we see him in a sympathetic light. His tirade against the shortcomings of his age does not reveal any desire to change the order of things. Rather, it is the talk of a good man angry at the world. Karl decides to become a robber only after everything he looked forward to seems lost. His decision is a transitory, emotional response evoked by wounded feelings and keen disappointment.

To justify his criminal undertakings to himself, Karl constructs an elaborate, rational fantasy that stars him as the hero of the shining blade who smites asunder the corrupt. In his mind, the men under his command are not common outlaws. They are idealistic vigilantes who punish those who abuse the law with impunity because of their powerful social position. There is a scene in the fourth act that shows his attitude vividly. Before sending his men to avenge his father, he orders them to kneel while he describes their mission as a holy, purifying act. He pronounces a blessing over their heads. They are crusaders, and he, the right hand of Providence, absolves them of their guilt (IV, 5). Karl believes that so long as he thinks and acts within a framework of noble ideals, his conscience will not bother him. Yet he suffers. Why? Because when ideals are translated into reality, they usually get soiled in the process. They lose their purity and become fallible, get infected by chance and circumstance. In Karl's ideal vision, society profits from the wrongs he rights. But in reality he causes more harm than good. Ideally, his men are above any interest in material gain, but in reality all but a handful lead this life because they are confirmed criminals. Later Karl is revolted to learn that a few even enjoy the killing. Disappointed and sick at heart, disjointed and weighed down with guilt, he pilgrimages to the site of earlier happiness.

Karl knows quite well that a visit home will be a painful experience. That he goes anyway leads us to suspect that he seeks self-punishment, as for example in the scene where he and Amalia walk in the picture gallery. Their conversation takes place on two levels. On the surface Karl pretends to be a traveling young nobleman with an interest in genealogy. Below the surface he experiences the agony of being with Amalia while knowing that their love has no future. But this pain is apparently insufficient. For when she wants to hurry past Karl's picture, he calls her back with questions, opening wounds.

The theme of self-punishment figures prominently in Karl's great insight in act 5. His already weak faith in the moral quality of his undertakings receives a mortal blow when he discovers that his disinheritance, his life as a robber, his crimes, and his regret are only the outgrowth of Franz's villainy, and that the hand of Providence had not selected him to do great deeds. The magnitude of his delusion staggers him: "O über mich Narren, der ich wähnete die Welt durch Greuel zu verschönern, und die Gesetze durch Gesetzlosigkeit aufrecht zu halten" ("What a fool I was to think that I could make the world a better place with horror and to uphold the law by breaking it," V, 2). This insight, along with the spectacle of his father, his brother, Amalia, and Schweitzer lying dead, and beholding the fragments of his own shattered life precipitate his decision to give himself up.

We can say that Karl surrenders to the authorities because remorse and guilt have made existence unendurable for him. He knows that the only way to gain peace of mind is to punish himself for his crimes. When he chooses to endure the punishment prescribed by law, he not only expiates the crimes but he also purifies himself. Self-punishment becomes his means of redemption.

Schiller makes Karl's death a noble one not only because he expiated his crimes but also because they were not motivated by personal gain. The principal characters in Schiller's drama who transgress because of self-interest, by contrast, die a squalid death—like Fiesko.

II   Die Verschwörung des Fiesko zu Genua

After the success of *Die Räuber,* Schiller began to make clandestine trips to Mannheim. Eventually the duke, who took a personal interest in the lives of his subjects, heard of Schiller's secret life. In August 1782 he ordered the young poet to cease not only his trips but also his literary activities. Since Schiller had already decided to become a writer, he deserted the army and fled to Mannheim, where he expected to work with Dalberg. The desertion frightened Dalberg because the duke was a powerful man whose influence extended beyond his own frontiers. Fearing unpleasant consequences, he refused to become involved. Accordingly, he rejected Schiller's new play *Die Verschwörung des Fiesko zu Genua,* claiming that it was unsuitable for the stage in its present form. He suggested extensive revisions. Yet when Schiller handed him a second version, he refused it as well. Later when he discovered that the duke intended to ignore Schiller, he relented and offered him the position of resident dramatist. In 1783 Schiller revised *Fiesko*, giving it its third and present form. Its first performance at Mannheim on 11 January 1784 was a failure, primarily because the protagonists lack the color, the magnetism, and the idealistic fervor which made *Die Räuber* such a success.

Schiller's first historical play, *Fiesko* dramatizes an event that took place at Genoa, Italy, in the year 1587. At that time the city was an independent republic which had been established by Andrea Doria in 1528. Many of the city's leading families, however, disliked this form of government and advocated a return to the old order. This faction found a leader in the wealthy, powerful, and popular Count Fiesko, who eventually led a successful conspiracy to overthrow Doria. But just as the count was to assume power, he visited the harbor to inspect some navy vessels anchored there, slipped on the gangway, fell into the sea, and drowned. Schiller dramatizes these events not as they actually happened but as they might have happened. In order to accommodate the requirements of good drama, he alters virtually every fact. Most obviously, he makes Fiesko a champion of the republic who gradually turns into an egotist hungry for power.

A   *The Elements of the Plot*

In the play, Andrea Doria is an old man of eighty who, though living in semiretirement, is still the most powerful and respected man in Genoa. He has delegated power and the daily business of government to Gianettino Doria, his nephew and heir, a blackguard who plots to abolish the republic and rule despotically. His dictatorial manner has already alienated many of the city's families. Yet they are powerless because the Dorias control the army and the navy. Count Fiesko, a brilliant young man of twenty-three, forms a conspiracy to topple the Dorias and save the republic. In secret and unknown to others he enlists the aid of foreign powers, which provide him with money, men, and ships. To divert suspicion, Fiesko constructs an elaborate deception pretending to lead the wanton life of a libertine. Part of his plan requires indifference toward his wife, Leonore, and the simulation of a hopeless infatuation for Julia Doria, Gianettino's sister and his equal in evil. The citizens cannot understand his fascination for her, so they conclude that nothing worthwhile can be expected from him—which is precisely what he wants them to think. Now after months of preparation, everything is ready for the armed revolt to begin. Schiller picks up the thread at this point.

At the beginning of act 1, Gianettino hires Hassan, a Moor from Tunis and professional assassin, to murder Fiesko. Yet when Hassan makes his attack, Fiesko wrests the dagger from him. With the blade now at the murderer's throat, he learns the identity of his employer. In an unlikely development, the two discover a mutual liking for each other. Seeing how Hassan's connections with the underworld can be useful to his plans, Fiesko engages his services. Meanwhile, Gianettino continues his outrages. He decides to deliver a humiliating blow to his chief republican adversary, Verrina, by raping his daughter. When the old man discovers the identity of the perpetrator, he swears revenge. He and three others launch a conspiracy of their own to kill Gianettino and free Genoa.

In act 2 Verrina and his conspirators pay a visit to Fiesko in an effort to enlist his support. They remember that before his romance with Julia he was the brightest star in the republican camp. Once they have stated their business, Fiesko throws off his disguise with a flourish and reveals to them the scope of his activities. The conspirators join forces. The act ends with a monologue in which Fiesko, highly agitated, considers his options: he can either seize the opportunity to subvert the conspiracy and crown himself duke, or he can support the republic. It is a great thing, he says, to seize a crown but it is divine to refuse one. He decides for the republic.

As the curtain rises upon act 3, Verrina is explaining to Bourgognino, his future son-in-law and fellow conspirator, that as soon as the Dorias are defeated, he will murder Fiesko. Verrina is certain that the count is merely pretending republicanism and that he in fact means to usurp the power for himself. Verrina's suspicions are proved correct in the very next scene where Fiesko stands at the window of his palace watching the sun rise over Genoa. He perceives himself in the midst of a great metaphor. Like the sun, the brilliance of his greatness floods the city with light. Unable to resist the tempting vision of himself as absolute ruler, he reverses his decision of the previous evening. He decides to subvert the revolt and put himself upon the throne. From this point on his actions are oriented in that direction. The idea of his own magnificence causes a remarkable change in his character; he affects a heroic gait, speaks imperiously, and acts callously.

The change in Fiesko's character first surfaces in his relationship to Hassan. Since employing a well-known assassin does not coincide with the image of himself as a legend in his own time, he tells the Moor that he does not wish to detain him in Genoa any longer. As he turns to walk away, he drops a sack of severance pay on the floor. Since Hassan feels affection for Fiesko, his feelings are wounded. He leaves with vengeance in his heart.

By the beginning of act 4 Fiesko's troops and the conspirators have assembled at his palace. The military coup will be launched that night. Suddenly the news arrives that Hassan has betrayed Fiesko to Andrea Doria. The conspirators are thrown into a panic. In a surprise development, Doria orders Hassan bound and sent to Fiesko with a note saying that he does not believe a word the Moor said. Furthermore, he intends to sleep without a bodyguard that night. Doria's generosity crushes Fiesko, for he cannot endure the spectacle of anyone exceeding him in nobility of gesture. He yearns to act even more nobly by aborting the revolt. After a brief argument, the others succeed in persuading him to abandon the idea. Still chafing, Fiesko later goes to Doria's house in disguise, stands in the street, and shouts warnings at his bedroom window. Now confident of success and so no longer needing his mask, Fiesko proves in a dramatic way that he has only been pretending indifference toward Leonore. He does so by humiliating Julia publicly. Later Leonore begs Fiesko to abandon the conspiracy for her sake. Deaf to her pleas, he marches out in full armor to lead the revolt.

Act 5 recounts the events of the armed clash. Fighting erupts in the harbor and in the streets. Bourgognino finds Gianettino and kills him. Hassan is caught setting fires, and Fiesko orders him hanged. Meanwhile Leonore, fearing for her husband's life, leaves the palace to look for him. She comes upon Gianettino's scarlet cape and, wishing to disguise herself, puts it on. Mistaking his wife for Gianettino in the dark, Fiesko kills her with his sword. When he sees what he has done, he falls to his knees in shock. His grief is of short duration, however. It occurs to him that Providence is testing him. Has he the power to overcome this blow to his heart and fulfill his destiny, or will he despair? Fiesko arises and carries on heroically.

After the battle is won, Fiesko visits the harbor with Verrina to free the galley slaves in accordance with tradition. On the way, Verrina, who suspects Fiesko's secret ambition to become ruler, twice begs him to renounce the crown. Fiesko refuses curtly. When they are halfway up the gangway of the first ship, Verrina decides to save the republic by pushing Fiesko into the sea. The drama ends as Verrina leaves to make his peace with Andrea Doria.

B   *The Nature of Simulation*

Fiesko's metamorphosis from a champion of freedom to an aspiring dictator accords with Schiller's ideas about the corrupting influence of false semblance. He explores this subject in the early *Philosophy of Physiognomy* (1779) and later again in his essays on aesthetics and on poetry. Schiller claims that if we make a conscious effort at dissimulation, we eventually become what we pretend to be, because character is not static but dynamic. It grows and changes and responds to its physical and moral environment. The faculty for make-believe may be used to improve character or to worsen it. Pretending is good for us if it is aesthetic semblance; it is harmful if it is false semblance, simulation, because then we turn ourselves into deceivers. Fiesko illustrates this theory in that by acting basely he becomes base. Fiesko's plan to free Genoa calls for simulating moral decay. He wears this mask for seven months. He even retains it in the presence of his wife. His performance is so professional that he succeeds in convincing everyone, including himself. For such is the nature of false semblance that when he finally does remove the mask, the face is identical with it. He performs an act of distorted self-creation in which he transforms himself into the scoundrel he pretends to be. This explains Schiller's statement in the preface to the drama that Fiesko is "ein Opfer der Kunst und Kabale" ("a victim of artifice and intrigue"); not the victim of other people's artifice, but of his own, Fiesko destroys himself.

Though most of the changes in Fiesko's character occur before the dramatic action begins, the final transfiguration takes place in two monologues placed almost back to back. In the first, we see a glimmer of the old Fiesko, who concludes that it is a greater thing to renounce a crown than to seize one (II, 18). But this is only a momentary relapse made under the influence of Verrina's patriotic fervor. In the second scene, as he watches the sun rise above Genoa, we see Fiesko as he has become. He debates the moral quality of his undertaking and concludes that he stands above moral considerations because he is a great man. Yet his subsequent actions show that he wants to be free of all law, and of all restrictions, not in order to elevate Genoa to higher heights, but "all die kochenden

Begierden—all die nimmersatten Wünsche in diesem grundlosen Ozean unterzutauchen" ("to plunge all my boiling lusts and insatiable appetites into this bottomless ocean," III, 2.)[2] In this attitude he displays the characteristics which Schiller enumerates for the *fantast* in his essay on human types. The fantast, he says, is the perverted extreme of idealism. He abandons nature and all moral compulsion not for the sake of the unconditional but "um dem Eigensinne der Begierden und den Launen der Einbildungskraft desto ungebundener nachgeben zu können" ("to better indulge the wantoness of his desires and the whims of his imagination").[3]

There are several other instances that illustrate how the practice of deception has changed Fiesko for the worse. He dismisses Hassan in a way that wounds him needlessly and that provokes him to revenge. Likewise, his humiliation of Julia goes beyond decorum. Even though we can justify his action in the light of her attempt to poison Leonore, the pleasure which he derives from it reveals low-mindedness. Another example is Fiesko's reaction to Doria's noble gesture in act 4. When Fiesko's and Andreas's deeds are placed side by side, we see how artificial, even cheap, Fiesko looks in comparison. This is not the only occasion, however, where we observe ignoble behavior and bad form in him. In fact, the greater Fiesko's ego inflates the shabbier he acts. We see it in his humiliation of Julia and Hassan. We observe it when he mistakes his wife for Gianettino. Had he wished to act like a great man when he recognized the scarlet cape, he might have challenged his adversary to a fair fight and so would have recognized his wife. Instead, he attacks the figure from behind wütend ("raging") and so murders Leonore by mistake.

Fiesko's reaction to Leonore's death is the most vivid revelation of the basic changes wrought in his character. When he realizes whom he has killed, he appears to act out of character. The stage directions specify animallike behavior: "viehisch um sich hauend" ("lashing out like an animal"); "rascher und wilder" ("faster and wilder"). At one point he seizes Calcagno and pushes his face right down against Leonore's, ordering him to grieve for the woman whom he desired. Fiesko's unseemly conduct during these scenes is an early example of naive behavior provoked by surprise. We recall that such behavior is an involuntary reaction to a sudden turn of events. The person loses his self-control allowing the real self underneath the pretensions to emerge. For the spectator, the event is like suddenly opening a window into the psyche providing a view of what is there. Himself again, the person is shocked and dismayed at his behavior. Fiesko fulfills some but not all of the requirements specified. The discovery of his wife's body evokes the display of the distortions which his character has undergone. But he never returns to his senses. Instead of vanishing once again behind the mask, the distortion remains.

Leonore's death symbolizes the death of Fiesko as a human being and his rebirth as a *fantast*. Throughout the drama, she is the only person for whom he shows tenderness and genuine affection. Her death severs the last thread connecting him with humanity. Now when feeling dies, egotism rushes in to fill the void. From this point onward Fiesko sees himself only as a child of destiny who has withstood the supreme test and who now ascends into the realm of the immortals. There is no cause for the audience to lament Fiesko's death, because as a human being he is dead already.

One of Schiller's favorite themes is the hero who uses noble ideals to mask motives of personal profit. It figures prominently in Ferdinand von Walter's character, the hero of Schiller's next drama.

III   Kabale und Liebe

Schiller spent most of the year 1783 hiding from Duke Karl Eugen on the Bauerbach estate belonging to Frau von Wolzogen, who was one of his admirers. There he had the leisure to work on *Kabale und Liebe* which he completed shortly before Dalberg appointed him resident dramatist of the Mannheim Theater in July 1783. The drama appeared in book form in March 1784. In April it premiered at Mannheim.

Schiller wrote *Love and Intrigue* at a time when the injustices of the class system occupied many intellectuals. In the eighteenth century, European society still adhered to a caste system with the landed aristocracy and the clergy at the apex, the peasants and the workers at the bottom, and the bourgeoisie in between. A rigid code of laws defined one's station in life down to grooming and dress. There was a law, for instance, which made it a crime for anyone but a noblewoman to wear the hair full-length down the back. Another forbade anyone but the nobility to wear metal buckles upon the shoes. It goes without saying that intermarriage between classes was rare. Neither did one marry for love. Particularly among the aristocracy parents arranged unions for political or economic reasons. We can imagine the reaction on both sides if the scion of a noble family suddenly announces his intention to marry the daughter of a social inferior. This is the situation in *Kabale und Liebe*, Schiller's only drama with a middle class setting.

A   *The Elements of the Plot*

Three months before the dramatic action begins Ferdinand, son of the dukedom's powerful President von Walter, comes to take flute lessons from the musician Miller. Miller has a beautiful daughter named Luise. Before long the two are deeply in love—much to the chagrin of a man named Wurm, the villain of the piece, who wants Luise for himself. Schiller takes up the action when Wurm decides to break up the relationship between Luise and Ferdinand. Since he is President von Walter's private secretary, he informs him that his son intends to marry beneath his station (I, 5). Concerned, the president devises a scheme to prevent the misalliance. Circumstances are favorable. The duke is getting married soon, a situation which could threaten the president's position. Furthermore, the arrival of the new duchess means that something will have to be done about the duke's mistress, Lady Emilie Milford. The president knows that if he can arrange a marriage between his son and Lady Milford, he will be doing his sovereign a favor. Instead of losing influence, he will increase it.

The manner in which the president informs his son of his future reveals his moral degradation (I, 7). To him Ferdinand is not a son, but a useful tool in the struggle for power. He begins the interview by recalling the sacrifices he has made for him, asking rhetorically for whom he committed all the murders and the crimes. For whom has he made infinite sacrifices? Why, for Ferdinand, of course, and now it is time for him to show his gratitude by marrying the duke's mistress. For this, he will be rewarded with riches and power. But Ferdinand refuses indignantly. His honor is at stake. He begs his father not to degrade him before the world. The president then tests his son by proposing another union with a woman of good reputation. When Ferdinand refuses this match too, he proves that it is marriage to Luise that he wants. To escape his father's wrath, Ferdinand agrees to keep an appointment with Lady Milford.

The Milford episode, though extraneous to the main line of the action, constitutes an important subplot. During the meeting with her, Ferdinand is surprised to learn that in private she is not at all the vain coquette she seems in public. He discovers that she is a person of high moral character who secretly uses her position to alleviate much suffering among the people. During the conversation we see that she understands her position at court. She knows that a few changes are necessary if things are to stay the way they are. She proposes a marriage in which they will both work together to make the dukedom a better place; besides, she has loved and admired Ferdinand secretly for some time. Although Ferdinand completely changes his mind about Lady Milford, he still intends to marry Luise. He will marry her even if it means losing everything and fleeing the country.

Upset over Ferdinand's refusal, Milford decides to break up the relationship between Ferdinand and Luise in her own way. She invites Luise to her private apartments in the palace. Then she dresses in her finest clothes. When Luise arrives, Milford affects the air of the suave lady of the world and connoisseur of sensual delights. This she does hoping to make Luise envious enough that she cannot refuse the offer to serve as Mylady's personal attendant: all these luxuries and special privileges she will give to Luise if she will but follow her and renounce Ferdinand. Luise refuses. According to Schiller's scheme of things, when innocence and deception collide, the former unmasks the latter. Mylady suddenly sees herself in perspective and feels shame for the first time. Immediately after the interview she walks out of the palace and vanishes.

Returning now to the main line of the plot, we find that the president is seriously worried about his son's plans. First he tries to separate the lovers by force (II, 6). When that fails, he and Wurm resort to kidnapping and extortion. The president orders Miller and his wife sent to prison. Wurm then tells Luise that she can free her parents by writing a false letter of love to a local dandy in which she describes her impatience for another tryst and mocks Ferdinand. Then Wurm makes her swear a sacred oath to secrecy, knowing that she is naive enough to keep her word. Then they play this letter into Ferdinand's hands, counting on his hot-headed jealousy to do the rest. At first everything works according to plan. But the scheme goes awry because Ferdinand in his despair poisons Luise and himself (V, 7). As she dies, she reveals the truth about how the love letter was extorted from her. Just before Ferdinand dies, the president and Wurm burst into the house. Enraged at the turn of events, the president publicly denounces Wurm as the guilty party. But Wurm shouts that he will reveal all the president's crimes with written proofs. Overwhelmed by his son's dying gesture of forgiveness, the president is transformed. As the curtain falls, he is ready to take the punishment for his crimes.

B   Naïve and Artificial Morality

Schiller's play is a general indictment of political and moral corruption in the eighteenth century. As he depicts it, the typical court is a battleground of greed, avarice, and brutal struggles for power. The participants are not ruled by culture and self-control, but by egoism and the urge for power, profit, and privilege, success going to the one who has the strength and the roguery to seize his opportunity. The president represents the professional politician. He is proud of his cunning. He relates with relish the story of how he gained power by blowing up his predecessor's house after first going there as a friend to an all-night drinking party to give himself the best alibi.

In contrast to this group stands Luise who embodies traditional virtues. She displays human warmth, heartfelt emotion, and consideration for others. Hard work, simple pleasures, and satisfaction with her condition are her qualities. She is honest, straightforward, natural, naïve. Whatever she says and does is the expression of a nature at one with itself. We see her qualities throughout the drama, but most clearly in her confrontation with Lady Milford, which represents an encounter between the natural and the artificial. Luise's uncorrupted simplicity has a remarkable effect upon Lady Milford which accords with what the author says about the way the person of sentimental temperament reacts to naive behavior. Milford is reminded of her own lost innocence and realizes what she has become. For years she had no difficulty in keeping the mask she wears at court from infecting her real self. But when she sees how artificial she looks next to Luise's natural simplicity, she gains perspective and realizes that she is, in fact, in danger of turning into the vain and morally decadent courtesan she pretends to be. When she understands this truth about herself she is able to change her life. She voluntarily gives up her position at court and vanishes. In the encounter between the two women nature triumphs over artifice and the spectator experiences moral pleasure.

The difference between Luise and Lady Milford can be made clearer if we examine their meeting in the light of Schiller's theory of active sublimity. We recall that there are two kinds of sublimity. If a person acts freely according to moral principles in the face of great temptation and despite undesirable consequences such a decision might bring, then we have a morally sublime act. Aesthetic sublimity, on the other hand, occurs whenever the hero regrets an action and expiates it freely. Luise is an example of the former when she withstands the pressure to compromise her values. She is a middle-class version of Leonidas at Thermopylae who stands by her virtue. Lady Milford, on the other hand, exemplifies aesthetically sublime behavior. She regrets her decision to become the prince's concubine, as well as her morally sordid life at court. To purify herself, she chooses to abandon everything and to endure the hardship, the uncertainties, and the anxieties of the outside world. Not only does the spectator experience moral pleasure at the spectacle of principles winning over passion but he also admires her as aesthetic object.

Ferdinand occupies a position between the naive and the sentimental, between the bourgeoisie and the aristocracy. He shares elements of each but he is at home in neither. Growing up surrounded by corruption, he is at first intrigued by and then infatuated with Luise's natural simplicity. Furthermore, he gains our admiration not only because he rebels against artificiality but also because we naturally admire someone who does what he thinks is right despite the hardship it may bring. He also engages our affection because he is in love. Yet we cannot overlook the fact that he rebels only when his personal wishes are thwarted, and that he cannot control his impulsive nature.

Ferdinand is another of Schiller's self-contradictory idealists who are motivated by selfish interests. He justifies his rebellion against his father on idealistic grounds, yet at the same time we see that his idealism is selectively applied. He knows about his father's long list of crimes, but he sees nothing wrong in owing his major's uniform to his father's influence. Neither does he hesitate to spend the tainted money on music lessons. Nor until now has he felt any urge to denounce his father as a criminal. He proclaims the worth and dignity of the individual but is oblivious to the spectacle of seven thousand soldiers sold to America. He claims that marriage to Lady Milford violates his honor, but this is simply an excuse because he wants to marry Luise. He demands the right to lead his own life, but he acts as Luise's judge, jury, and executioner. We can therefore say that Ferdinand's idealism is too colored by self-interest to justify our admiration.

Sometimes *Kabale und Liebe* is compared to Shakespeare's *Othello* in that both dramas involve villains, love, intrigue, jealousy, as well as the murder and the suicide of lovers. The similarities, however, are only superficial. In Schiller's drama the catastrophe is caused more by Ferdinand's personality than by the villain Wurm. Acting from malignant hatred, Iago destroys a strong man by manipulating the weakest part of his character. Ferdinand has an impulsive, overzealous, weak character which proves unable to cope with circumstances demanding self-discipline. Othello commits suicide because he is disappointed in himself, Ferdinand because he is disappointed in Luise. Iago spins his web artfully, whereas the president and Wurm are heavy-handed.

Kabale und Liebe is Schiller's most realistic play. The plot, the characterization, and the colorful language give it a colloquial flavor. Each figure speaks in his own idiom which, in turn, suits his station in life. Miller's conversation around the house is heavily laden with street and shop jargon frequently approaching the unsavory. But he elevates his language along with his behavior when he talks to Ferdinand or to the president. Frau Miller whines, Luise gushes. The president speaks in grandiose imperatives which reflect his authoritarian personality, Wurm speaks obsequiously, and Hofmarschall von Kalb's empty-headed chatter goes with his role as court gossip.

After *Kabale und Liebe* Schiller wrote no other drama using everyday language because he changed his views about art. From now on he would be interested in solemn tragedy and in heroic action which requires a uniform level of style. His next drama, *Don Carlos*, reflects the new direction.

IV   Don Carlos

Late in the year 1783 Schiller received Gottfried Körner's generous invitation to join him at his home in Leipzig. At first Schiller did not reply. But when Dalberg did not renew his contract in August 1784, he became desperate for a job. With creditors pressing and no prospects for the future, he accepted the invitation. He arrived at Leipzig in April 1785. Körner's patronage allowed Schiller to concentrate on his writing. The chief dramatic product of this period is *Don Carlos*, which he had begun in 1783 and which was published in June 1787. It premiered the following August in Hamburg. Next, it played successfully in Mannheim and in Berlin.

Schiller researched the material for his second historical drama carefully. He read a German translation of Robert Watson's *History of Philip II* (1778) and translated Mercier's factual account *Portrait de Philippe II* (1785) into German. He published this translation in his literary journal *Die Thalia* along with the first three acts of the play (1786). These and other historical accounts relate that Crown Prince Don Carlos was mentally unbalanced. He entertained an unnatural hatred for his father, had a mercurial temper, and had a passion for torturing small animals. Finally in 1568, realizing that his son was a threat to the state, Philip II ordered him imprisoned in a room in the palace. The stress of confinement exacerbated the prince's unbalanced mind, and he died the same year of overeating.

In addition to the historical facts, Schiller was also familiar with the many bizarre legends and rumors which flourished for two centuries after Don Carlos's death. One of the legends involves revolution and the Inquisition. Another suggests a love affair between Philip's wife Elizabeth and Carlos. Many believed that Philip killed his son from jealousy. Eventually, a man named César Vichard Saint-Real spun these legends into a French romance entitled *Don Carlos, Nouvelle Historique* (1672), which Schiller also read. As it is his custom, the poet in his play tells the historical events not as they were, but as they might have been. He retains Carlos's dislike of his father, his mercurial temperament, his passion for Elizabeth, and Philip's role in his death. The most important addition is the Marquis Posa and his ideal of freedom.

A   The Elements of the Plot

In order to summarize the plot, we must go back several years before the dramatic action begins. When Crown Prince Don Carlos was a little boy, he loved Roderick, the young marquis of Posa, more than anything in the world. He followed him wherever he went, imitated him, and wanted to be his friend. But the marquis ignored him. Then one day at play, the marquis's shuttlecock accidentally struck the visiting queen of Bohemia in the eye. Convinced that the children did it on purpose, King Philip called them together to discover and to punish the culprit. On impulse Carlos stepped forward, declared himself the guilty party, and took the marquis's thrashing. Moved by this sublime gesture, Posa became Carlos's inseparable friend. Strong and charismatic, Posa dominates the weaker Carlos from the very beginning of their relationship. He communicates his dream of an ideal society to the young prince, convincing him that freedom is the prerequisite.

Posa and Carlos attend the University of Alcala. After graduation Posa embarks upon a two-year journey through Europe. The

purpose of the trip, which he keeps a secret even from his friend, is
to enlist the aid of foreign powers in a plan to topple Philip from
power and place Carlos on the throne. Then they will create a new
society based on idealistic principles that are nearly utopian.

While Posa intrigues, the beautiful Elizabeth de Valois is chosen
as the prince's future bride. The political arrangement soon blos-
soms into love. But when Philip's wife dies, the king decides to
marry Elizabeth himself. Carlos's passion persists. More often than
not dreams of a clandestine affair replace visions of the Golden Age.
Such is Carlos's state of mind when Posa returns from his successful
expedition. Schiller takes up the action of the drama upon Posa's
arrival at court.

At their first meeting the only subject Carlos wishes to discuss
with Posa is his love for Elizabeth. When Posa reminds him of their
plans for Spain's future, Carlos dismisses them as youthful fantasies.
Carlos's attitude alarms Posa, for the success of the rebellion
depends on Carlos's active participation. An expert in human
nature, Posa decides to exploit Carlos's passion to further the cause
of freedom. Posa asks Elizabeth, whom he knows to be sympathetic
to the cause, to grant her son-in-law an interview for the purpose of
asking him to work for the liberation of the Netherlands. Posa also
knows that Elizabeth as a person of high moral standards will thwart
Carlos's desire for an intimate relationship. The stratagem works
and Carlos returns rededicated to political freedom.

In the end Posa's efforts to redirect Carlos's passion prove futile.
For unknown to both, Carlos's love for Elizabeth evokes a reaction
from the Princess Eboli, lady-in-waiting to the queen, that ultimately thwarts the rebellion, leads to the downfall of Posa and
Carlos, and destroys the queen. It all happens because Eboli
accidentally intercepts a note from Carlos to the queen. Thinking
herself the object of his affection, she invites him to a trysting place.
Carlos keeps the rendezvous because he believes that the invitation
comes from the queen. The misunderstanding is clarified only after
Carlos awkwardly rejects her advances. Humiliated, Eboli concludes
falsely that he and the queen are lovers and swears vengeance upon
both of them. Her first step is to cooperate with Domingo and the
duke of Alba, two courtiers striving for political power at any price.
The three launch a complex intrigue which involves fabricating
evidence to make Philip believe that his son and his wife are lovers
and that his very own daughter is the offspring of this incestuous
union. The plan requires Eboli to become Philip's concubine so that

she can give him stolen love letters from Carlos to the queen. Although the letters date from the time of their legal engagement, she tells the king that they are of current origin, and he believes her.

Depressed, pondering revenge, and suffering from loneliness late one night, the king accidentally notices the marquis of Posa's name on the list of exceptional people which he customarily keeps on his desk. Since he can recall neither the name nor the circumstances, Philip summons him to a private meeting in his study. No one is more surprised at the honor than Posa, for long ago he dismissed the king as a narrow-minded despot from whom nothing worthwhile can be expected. Nevertheless, he decides to take advantage of the opportunity and perhaps gain something for the cause.

The encounter between the visionary idealist and the cynical realist ranks among the most famous scenes of German drama (III, 10). The force of Posa's personality surprises both the audience and the king. Instead of the monarch overawing the young nobleman, it is the other way around. Posa immediately takes charge of the conversation and deftly leads it in the direction he wants it to go. First he refuses the king's service. He can be no part of a crown policy, he says, that aims at keeping the citizen in a state of mindless submission. Then, speaking from the heart, he describes his vision of noble humanity. He likens men to gods and pleads the case for human dignity. Finally he falls on his knees and begs for freedom of thought, speaking the famous line: *"O. Geben Sie Gedankenfreiheit"* ("Oh, Give us Freedom of thought").

The marquis impresses the king greatly. Moreover, he has come at precisely the right moment, for the king needs a friend. Since Posa is the only man whom he has ever respected, he virtually orders him to be his best and only friend. The feeling is not mutual, however. As subsequent events show, Posa despises the king, uses him, and finally betrays him. In fact, he begins to manipulate the monarch at once. Posa leads him to believe that Carlos is a possible security risk and that for that reason Philip should give him a secret warrant of arrest as a contingency measure. He complies, and Posa leaves the room as the most powerful man in Spain.

Shortly after Posa leaves, Elizabeth surprises Philip with the angry complaint that someone has broken into her strongbox and has stolen some letters from Prince Carlos to her. Philip reacts violently. He accuses her of infidelity and incest in the most abusive way. Stunned by her husband's savage outburst, she faints, gashing her head as she falls. Once Philip regains his senses, he is ashamed of his behavior. In this state he agonizes until Posa earns his undying gratitude by exposing Eboli's intrigue and proving that both his wife and his son are innocent of all charges.

The news of Elizabeth's mistreatment spreads rapidly with unfortunate results for Posa and the rebellion. Ignorant of the circumstances and alarmed for the queen's safety, Carlos impulsively rushes to Eboli's apartment with frantic pleas for an audience with the queen. Suspicious, Posa follows him with some guards, arriving just in time to see him on his knees before Eboli (IV, 16). Wrongly concluding that Carlos has told her about the rebellion, and taken unawares by this sudden turn of events, Posa appears to act out of character. He quickly produces the warrant of arrest and orders Carlos seized. Then he grasps Eboli with the firm intention of dispatching her with his dagger when he conceives of a nobler alternative.

Realizing that he has jeopardized the rebellion himself by this precipitous action, Posa sees that he can nevertheless guarantee its success by sacrificing his life to it. The idea appeals to him, and he makes a plan. He composes a self-incriminating letter to William of Orange—leader of the Dutch revolt—in which he mocks Philip, announces that he is the queen's lover, and ends by saying that he is leaving for Flanders. He arranges for this letter to fall into Philip's hands, knowing that Philip is the kind of man who will order his execution for this betrayal. Posa plans for the shock of his death to inspire Carlos to escape to Flanders and lead the revolt. The subterfuge works for awhile. While Posa waits for the news of his betrayal to reach Philip, he visits Carlos in his cell. Carlos understands when his friend tells him that even though he deceived and manipulated him, it was for a noble purpose. While they talk, a shot rings out and Posa falls dead (V, 3).

Before Carlos fully realizes what has happened, the king arrives at the cell with his retinue to free him. There follows a brutal scene in which the son succeeds in humiliating his father, who collapses unconscious into the arms of Domingo and Alba. Meanwhile, the queen has taken action of her own by instigating a general uprising in the streets of Madrid as a diversionary tactic to allow Carlos to escape in the confusion. When the news of the disturbance arrives at the dungeon, everyone rushes out. A secret messenger arrives from the queen to tell Carlos that she has a message for him from Posa and that she will expect him in her chambers at midnight. He is to disguise himself as Charles V to get by the guards, for superstition has it that the ghost of the departed monarch often wanders abroad at night. Later that day, the king discovers his heir's involvement in the conspiracy. It is clear to Philip that for reasons of state, his son must die—preferably through the Inquisition. Philip decides to summon the grand inquisitor.

The grand inquisitor is an old man of ninety and blind, Schiller's image of religious oppression and intolerance. The king is startled to learn that for years the inquisitor has been grooming Posa for a sacrificial death. He explains that since reason and the spread of freedom in Europe has undermined the church's power over the minds of its subjects, the church must regain it by degrading a symbol of freedom and reason "Durch uns zu sterben, war er da. Ihn schenkte / Der Notdurft dieses Zeitenlaufes Gott, / In seines Geistes feierliche Schändung / Die prahlende Vernunft zur Schau zu führen. / Das war mein überlegter Plan." ("To die for us was his excuse for living. / God granted him unto this epoch's need / To make of swaggering Reason an example / By formal degradation of his mind. / That was my well considered plan," V, 10).[4] He is disgusted at the king's behavior in this whole affair. Not only is the monarch guilty of stealing church property, he has not acted like a monarch at all, but like a human being who needs warmth and affection. Has he forgotten the first rule of statecraft, the inquisitor asks, that the man of authority must value nothing that can be denied to him? How could a man of his experience allow himself to be seduced by the freedom fantasies of the world reformer? Has he not learned that freedom and stability are inconceivable together? And what of consistency? How can Philip sign the death warrant of a hundred thousand sinners and then exempt the most dangerous man alive? Systematic oppression is the only way to maintain law and order.

After Philip has endured several minutes of reproach, he asks the inquisitor if he will preside over his son's execution. The inquisitor agrees if Philip submits to the authority of the church. Together they go to the queen's chamber, where they know Carlos to be. They arrive there just in time to observe them in a farewell embrace. The curtain falls as the king turns his son over to the Inquisition and a sacrificial death.

B   *The Idealist as Perpetrator of Evil*

The distressing thing about Posa is that he acts with such a clear conscience. He manipulates Carlos, betrays the king's trust, hurts the queen, and plots rebellion, all without experiencing remorse. And he could have killed Eboli without feeling anything. Yet we know him to be a person of noble principles. The question is, How can he be two things at once? How can he pursue a merciful idea mercilessly, trample underfoot the very humanistic principles that he champions, and then not see what he is doing? The answer is that he is an idealist and thus believes that the means justify the end. As we recall from Schiller's essay on poetry, he divided human beings into two groups: idealists and realists. Posa serves to illustrate the former, Philip the latter.

Like the idealist in Schiller's theoretical model, Posa exalts reason. For him reason is the source of all values, the basis of all judgment, the cause and the justification of all endeavor. Emotion is to be transcended because it is limited and transitory, whereas what reason produces is unlimited, incorruptible, and eternal. For him there are no limits to what man can make of himself with the help of his rational faculty. The noblest product of Posa's mind is the idea that within every human there slumbers an archetypal image of ideal man. Since man requires freedom to realize that ideal image, Posa will provide it at any price. If the betterment of mankind cannot be achieved lawfully, the idealist feels justified, even obligated, to employ unlawful and unscrupulous means. The same applies to personal relationships: friends and foes alike are manipulated for the sake of the cause.

Several instances illuminate Posa's one-sided view of the world. The first occurs at the beginning of the play when he and Carlos meet after the long separation. Ordinarily, we might expect the two friends to rejoice in the reunion. But this is not the case. Instead of a genuine encounter we face one dominated by Posa's sense of mission. As soon as Carlos begins to unburden his heart, Posa draws himself up stiffly to inform him that it is not Roderick who stands here, "nicht als des Knaben Carlos Spielgeselle— / Ein Abgeordneter der ganzen Menschheit / Umarm ich Sie—es sind die Flandrischen / Provinzen, die an Ihrem Halse weinen" ("nor the playmate of the boy-prince Carlos,— / As a deputy of all humanity / I now embrace you, and it is the Flemish / Provinces that weep upon your neck," I, 20). In other words, personal feelings take second place to the cause. Then as soon as Posa discovers that Carlos's infatuation with the queen might imperil the rebellion, he uses dubious means to gain control. Schiller tells us in his *Letters on Don Carlos* that Posa's main objective should have been to calm the prince's passion.[5] Instead, he encourages it because he sees a way of turning Carlos's passion for the queen into a passion for the revolt.

Even more revealing is that episode from early life when Carlos took Posa's thrashing. Posa regards it as a rite of initiation in which the prince proves that he is worthy to join the proud and the elect. Afterwards, Posa bestows upon the prince his admiration and his friendship as if awarding a medal: "Mein Stolz ist überwunden. / Ich will bezahlen wenn du König bist." ("My pride is overcome. / I shall repay the debt when you are King," I, 2). But now that Posa is a grown man, he does not desire to postpone until the coronation that which can be achieved sooner. If the rebellion succeeds, Posa will be kingmaker. He can crown Carlos and so discharge his obligations and at the same time put Carlos in debt to him. This ranks among the main reasons for Posa's decision to deceive and then to destroy King Philip.

Posa reveals yet another dimension of his idealist character in his meeting with Philip. His performance is a brilliant piece of deception. On the surface he pretends straightforwardness, honesty, and respect. Underneath, he is saying something like this: Philip, you are a narrowminded tyrant in the worst sense of the word. I despise you and everything that you stand for. But my ideal comes first. So I am going to suppress my loathing for you and win your confidence. I shall flatter you most subtly. I am going to take everything I hate about you and call it virtue. I shall take the negative and make it positive. I shall turn wrong into right and glorify you. Your opinion of humanity disgusts me, but I will say: "Die Menschen zwangen Sie dazu; *die* haben / Freiwillig ihres Adels sich begeben, / Freiwillig sich auf diese niedre Stufe / Herabgestellt" ("Human beings forced you to it; *they* / Of their own free will sold their nobility, / of their free will reduced themselves to this / Base level" III, 10). Although I know you to be ignorant of human nature, I shall call you "der erfahrne Kenner / In Menschenseelen." ("the experienced knower / Of human souls"). I still shudder thinking about the charred bones of those men burned on your orders in Flanders, but I shall pretend awe and praise your will power: "Sie müssen. Dass Sie können, / Was Sie zu müssen eingesehn, hat mich / Mit schauernder Bewunderung durchdrungen. / O Schade, dass, in seinem Blut gewälzt, / Das Opfer wenig dazu taugt, dem Geist / Des Opferers ein Loblied anzustimmen!" ("*You* had to. That you *can* / Do what you realized you had to, filled / Me with horrified admiration. / A pity that the victim drowned in his / Own blood

cannot intone a hymn of praise to / The spirit of the executioner!"').
Despite my disdain for you, I shall sympathize with your loneliness
and give you understanding: "*Sie* fuhren fort / Als Sterblicher zu
leiden, zu begehren; / *Sie* brauchen Mitgefühl" ("You went / On
suffering as a mortal, and desiring; / Now *you* need sympathy").
When I gain your confidence, I shall manipulate you. After you
have served my purposes, I shall take great pleasure in sacrificing
you to the cause. Posa's performance is so well done that he
completely deceives the king. He leaves the interview at the zenith
of his career.

Posa's decision to destroy the king is not an act of necessity, but
of choice. As a practical alternative he could have achieved many of
his aims and laid the foundation for others by taking advantage of
the king's admiration for him. Then when Carlos had ascended the
throne, they could have ushered in the new era. But Posa is just as
impatient and intoxicated with his ideal as Carlos is obsessed with
his passion for Elizabeth. These defects overtake Posa in act 4 when
Carlos' arrest commits him to action before the time is right.
Consequently, he loses control of the situation. To punish himself as
well as to save the cause, Posa decides on an act of sublime self-
sacrifice.

Posa's act of sublimity is different from the active and passive
types discussed in chapter 1. Posa sacrifices himself to ennoble an
ideal. Schiller says that Posa's deed is similar to the self-sacrifice of
the famous Spartan lawgiver Lycurgos. In that story, which Schiller
relates in the twelfth of his *Letters on Don Carlos*, Lycurgos
persuaded the Spartans to adopt his legal reforms. Then he left on a
long journey, but not before extracting from his fellow citizens a
promise to make no changes in the laws until his return. Then
Lycurgos left the city and starved himself to death. In his will he
specified that he be cremated and that his ashes be scattered to
prevent even a symbolical return. Lycurgos suspected, of course,
that his countrymen might not feel themselves bound to honor their
promise under such circumstances. But he knew that his sacrifice
would not be in vain; for in dying for his ideal, he gave the people
a sense of its value. Schiller observes that not only did he sanctify
his ideal, he ennobled himself too. Even today he is remembered as
a great man of history. Posa's death is similar to that of Lycurgos
with one exception. Whereas Lycurgos was concerned strictly with
his ideal, Posa has a keen desire to rank among the great benefactors
of mankind. The Queen appreciates the truth: "Sie haben / Nur um

Bewunderung gebuhlt" ("You only vied for admiration," IV, 21). Later Posa admits as much to Carlos: "Ja, soll / Ich dir's gestehen, Karl? Ich habe mich / Darauf gefreut" ("To tell the truth, shall I confess It to you, Charles? I had looked forward to it with pleasure," V, 3). We may therefore conclude that Posa dies not only for Carlos and the success of the revolt but also because he wants to be remembered as a great man.

In contrast to Posa's sublime self-sacrifice stands Princess Eboli, who displays aesthetic sublimity. The sequence of events culminating in her regeneration begins when she agrees to become the king's mistress so that she can use him to destroy Carlos and the queen. After the deed is done, she is racked by a guilty conscience. She discovers that she cannot look the queen in the face without feeling unwell. Life becomes painful for her. At one point she is so miserable that she begs the hesitating Posa to kill her: "Ich habe / Verdient zu sterben, und ich will's" ("I have / Deserved to die, and wish to," IV, 17). Yet as we know, pain of conscience can be extinguished only by voluntary self-punishment, which explains why Eboli confesses everything to the queen. She needs that agonizing experience to regain her peace of mind. She needs to writhe upon the floor in anguish and the punishment which is meted out to her. In acting according to the principle of self-forgiveness through self-punishment, Eboli regains her equilibrium. Her confession is an act of great courage that shows responsibility for her actions, which puts her in the same category with Schiller's other heroes and heroines who atone for past transgression through voluntary suffering.

C *The Realist*

As Posa illustrates the characteristics of the idealist, so King Philip demonstrates those of the realist. For him, all knowledge, action, and all rules of judgment are based on observation and experience. Consequently, he views people only as they are in their limited and imperfect reality, not as they could, or ought to, be. Since the only people he sees are courtiers like Alba, Domingo, and the grandees— sycophants who will do anything to enrich themselves—he believes that most men are like them; hence, humanity ranks low in Philip's estimation. He denies the individual intrinsic value. He does not ask if a person is good, only what he is good for. For him, the individual is something to be molded and used to a purpose. It matters little to Philip that Alba is a blackguard as long as he is useful: "Was sie verdienen, haben / Sie mir gegolten. Ihre zahmen Laster, / Beherrscht vom Zaume, dienen meinen Zwecken" ("As their merits are, so have / I valued them. Their tame little vices, / Checked by the reins, have served my purposes," III, 5). These are the values underlying Philip's world view.

We can imagine the king's initial shock and subsequent delight when he meets Posa—a man who is not for sale at any price. Like his son before him, Philip discovers that Posa's respect and friendship must be earned. Furthermore, Posa does not appear to act from any motive of gain. Instead of wealth and power, he asks for freedom of thought. Posa paints a fascinating picture of the ideal man to whom he wishes to give birth. Consequently, Philip believes that he has met someone who can give him friendship and truth. Realist that he is, he expresses his affection by showering Posa with gifts. Yet Posa does not give his friendship because he thinks that Philip is unworthy of it.

The sequence of events which justify Posa's low opinion of the monarch accords with the theory of naive behavior provoked by the unexpected. Philip reveals his true self in his reaction to Posa's letter to William of Orange. Unprepared for Posa's betrayal, he reacts instinctively and orders him shot. Philip's response corroborates Posa's opinion of him which Don Carlos sums up for his father: "Wie gering musst' er / Sie schätzen, da er's unternahm, bei Ihnen / Mit diesem plumpen Gaukelspiel zu reichen! / Um seine Freundschaft wagten Sie zu buhlen / Und unterlagen dieser leichten Probe!" ("What scorn he must have had / For you when undertaking to achieve / His ends with you by that crude artifice! / And you presumed to court his friendship, yet / You were inadequate to that slight test!" V, 4).

When Philip regains his senses, he is overwhelmed by remorse; not because he feels guilty but because Posa died with such a low opinion of him. He regrets that he cannot disprove Posa's judgment of him. In other words, his remorse stems from wounded pride rather than from breaking a moral law. Philip's subsequent deeds once again confirm Posa's judgment of him.

Philip emerges from the ordeal of Posa's betrayal a changed man, for in his heart darkness has won the victory over light, and vengeance has become the life force. If we could read his thoughts, they would run approximately as follows: "Posa, you have wounded me beyond endurance. I offered you my affection and my friendship.

You could have had anything. I was even willing to develop a new crown policy to accomodate your special talents. Never, never can I forgive you for the monstrous injustice that you have perpetrated upon me. And now I am going to take my revenge. I shall become your negative pole. I will take everything you loathed and proclaim it policy. You loved humanity? Well, I will grind it underfoot. You believed in Golden Ages? I will embalm man in the present. You loved freedom? I will throw man into spiritual servitude. You once told me how much you valued right conduct for its own sake, therefore I will attach reward and punishment to every word and deed and so cast humanity into the bondage of false values. You exalted the mind? I shall degrade it. You strove for the betterment of mankind? Very well, let mankind expiate the pain that you have inflicted upon me":

> Er sei gestorben als ein Tor. Sein Sturz
> Erdrücke seinen Freund und sein Jahrhundert!
> . . . .
>
> Dass nach mir
> Kein Pflanzer mehr in zehen Menschenaltern
> Auf dieser Brandstatt ernten soll. Er brachte
> Der Menschheit, seinem Götzen, mich zum Opfer;
> Die Menschheit büsse mir für ihn!—Und jetzt—
> Mit seiner Puppe fang' ich an.

> Let him have died a fool. And let his fall
> Drag down his friend and all his century.
> . . . .
>
> For ten human ages after me no sower
> Shall reap again this charred and fire swept field.
> He sacrificed me to humanity,
> His idol; let humanity atone
> For him.—and now—I shall start with his puppet.

(V, 9)

So Philip enlists the aid of the grand inquisitor.

The grand inquisitor is the true force of negation in this drama. He is an old man, blind, and desicated—like his ideas. He is contemptuous of humanity which he regards as an unruly mob of weak souls. According to the inquisitor, men are ruled by impulse and passion; hence, law and order can be maintained only through force, or through the threat of it. Freedom and social stability are incompatible, he says. Why? Because freedom is too heavy a burden upon man. Freedom requires self-discipline, subordination of self-interest to the good of the whole, and behavior according to moral principles. Since most men are venal and weak like Domingo, Alba, and the grandees, and incapable of highly principled action, they must be guided by a strong hand.

With the grand inquisitor, Schiller adds a total skeptic to his cast of human types. The inquisitor represents realism carried to its logical extreme. Schiller taunts his audience with a vision of a negating force which he himself totally rejected. Of course, he seems to say, the inquisitor is right about man in his present condition. It is probably true that a great many men are like the grandees and so get treated as they deserve. But the inquisitor is wrong to conclude that man's present reality is also his permanent condition. Man has another dimension. He exists also as a potential; he is a creature who can grow, change, develop, transcend himself. The inquisitor has committed the great error to which every realist is prone. He has taken a rule formulated on the basis of a particular observation and has elevated it to a universal law. His error consists in misreading nature. Nature works upon the concept of growth and freedom to change. Like nature, the individual and society are in an eternal state of becoming. The individual grows. Society grows. Civilizations are alive. It is natural to grow. In this philosophy, whatever promotes growth is the highest good and whatever prevents growth is the ultimate evil. Such forms of growth as creativity and discovery rely on the unpredictable-inspirational element in man that provides the impulse to disobey the urge of tradition in order to seek other alternatives. To create, man must begin by creating disorder. Tension between order and instability is a feature of change and a source of creativity. In each creative act man learns how things are put together, and in so doing he transcends his former self and affirms the principle of self-improvement. At the same time, growing individuals ensure the improvement of society as a whole, which progresses according to the cumulative creative efforts of its citizens. To deny the validity of unpredictability and change means to negate the mechanics by which civilizations go forward. But neither Philip nor the inquisitor are interested in progress or creativity: "Der Verwesung lieber, als / *Der* Freiheit" ("Putrefaction before / Freedom like *that,*" V, 10) are the words inscribed on their banner. Together they will inaugurate an era of unthinking obedience. Such is the lesson to be learned from this scene.

D   *The Necessity of Inner Balance*

Among the recurring themes in Schiller's drama is the ideal of psychic harmony. In one form or another, it underlies each of his plays. We have seen the results of psychic imbalance in Karl Moor, Fiesko, and Ferdinand; and we have seen equilibrium in Luise Miller. In *Don Carlos* the theme of a proper balance between reason and feeling is approached from several different directions. Posa, as we have seen, represents the consequences of overemphasizing reason. In the following remarks we shall discuss the destructive forces of emotion as illustrated by Carlos's behavior. In addition, we will offer the queen as an example of the harmonious interaction between reason and emotion.

Throughout the drama, Don Carlos is the victim of overpowering emotions which rule his life, shape his character, and contribute to his destruction. Furthermore, he is at the mercy of an overheated temperament. In the stage directions Schiller specifies for him a body language that highlights his emotionalism: "Er wirft sich stumm zu der Königin Füssen, steht dann rasch auf, und eilt ausser Fassung fort" ("He throws himself wordless at the Queen's feet, then gets up quickly, and rushes away overcome," II, 6); "Im Ausdruck der höchsten Empfindung" ("In the expression of the greatest emotion," II, 2); "Ausser Fassung durchs Zimmer stürzend und die Arme zum Himmel empor geworfen" ("He rushes about the room beside himself, his arms in the air," II, 4). When Carlos confronts the queen with his desires in the first act, she tells him "Sie rasen" ("you are raving wildly," I, 5). Philip, Alba, and the Princess Eboli all remark upon his unnatural behavior (II, 2, 3, 8).

Carlos's emotionalism manifests itself most apparently in the passionate attachment which he develops first for Posa and later for the queen. We remember that in early life Carlos was infatuated with Posa. He suffered the beating both to display his love and to compel the affection that he could not command. Carlos's behavior defines their future relationship which is not one between friend and friend but between student and master. Posa instructs him about the good, the beautiful, and the sublime. He educates him to see man's potential and to strive for the ideal. And Carlos, in his boundless efforts to please, becomes a copy of Posa. His enthusiasm for the ideal is artificial because he identifies the ideal with the person. This is why his idealism collapses when Posa leaves Spain. When he returns, the prince tells him that he has forgotten all about their childhood fantasies. Posa recognizes his friend immediately. He sees that the prince's passion for Elizabeth mirrors the earlier fixation that the prince had for him. Posa regains control by asking the queen to tell Carlos that she cares about Flanders, for Posa knows that Carlos in general idolizes whatever the object of his affection holds sacred. If Posa loves the ideal, so does Carlos. If the Queen honors freedom, so will he. Says Carlos to Posa after seeing Elizabeth: "Ich bin entschlossen. Flandern sei gerettet. / Sie will es—das ist mir genug" ("I have decided. Flanders shall be saved. / She wishes it.—That is enough for me," I, 7).

At the end of the drama, Carlos is free of his obsession for the queen and has rededicated himself to the cause of freedom. But this metamorphosis is not of his own construction. There has been no inner struggle, no sublime act of will, no rebirth into the realm of the immortals. Carlos has been shocked into this attitude by Posa's act of sublimity. The credit for the prince's change of mind therefore goes to Posa.

The bad effects of emotional preponderance are put into relief by the figure of Queen Elizabeth, who is Schiller's portrait of the ideal. She is an early example of what Schiller, following Goethe, later called "eine schöne Seele" ("a beautiful soul") in the essay *On Grace and Dignity*. In a beautiful soul there is no mind-body gap, no conflict between volition and duty, no agony of choice. Since Schiller calls such a person free, a more accurate—though less colorful—way of translating "eine schöne Seele" is "a free soul." As the representative of the ideal, Elizabeth is the only person in the drama who is well balanced; hence, she is also the only one who has not created an artificial self. She never feigns to be what she is not. Nor does she speak differently from what she thinks and feels; her display of passive sublimity makes her boundless.

In passive sublimity we overcome an impulse whose indulgence would violate a moral principle. We see this state of mind at work in her relationship to Carlos. We know that she has always loved him and she still does. But now that she is Philip's wife and therefore Carlos' mother, she cannot give form to her love: "Weil meine Pflicht—Unglücklicher, wozu / Die traurige Zergliederung des Schicksals, / Dem Sie und ich gehorchen müssen?" ("Because of my obligation—wretched man, / Why drearily anatomize the fate / Which you and I must still obey," I, 5). She refuses Carlos for another reason. To accept him as her lover, she would need to pretend fidelity to Philip and to the court, which means that she would have to create an artificial self. So she uses her willpower to conquer her inclination.

If the queen is such an enemy of simulation, then why does she become involved in Posa's scheme? Why does she consecrate Carlos's mission to Flanders and then create trouble in the streets so that he can escape in the confusion? Are her actions not treasonous? Does she not betray Philip and Spain? If she can dissemble on behalf of the rebellion, why can she not pretend for Carlos? Elizabeth rebels because it is a spontaneous reaction against an order that is false, perverted, and contrary to nature. For her, Spain is a land of barbaric customs and *autos da fé*, of cruel laws and intolerance, of men cowed in fear. She is willing to adjust herself to circumstances up to a point, for she is after all the queen of Spain and that position carries certain liabilities. Although she does not support her husband's policies in Flanders, she is reluctant to take action. When Posa attempts to enlist her support in act 2, she wants to consider the matter first. Her decision comes only when further compromise would mean to compromise her own nature.

Three events precipitate Elizabeth's rebellion. First, her husband participates in spying upon her which she regards as dishonorable. Second, Philip accuses her of adultery with his son in the most brutal way. In believing her guilty of infidelity, the "knower of human souls" proves that he does not even know his own wife. Because if he did he would know her incapable of that kind of duplicity. So, in misjudging her, he has revealed how basely he thinks of her. Third, she finds out from Eboli that he has accused her of adultery while engaging in it himself. In other words, the queen recognizes Philip for what he is. She therefore agrees to Posa's plan for one reason: it is natural to resist the unnatural.

Yet the queen is destroyed along with Carlos. Although Schiller does not tell us what happens after the curtain falls, we assume that the grand inquisitor will celebrate an *auto-da-fé à deux*.

CHAPTER 4

Drama of the Classical Period

TEN years elapsed between *Don Carlos* and the first drama of Schiller's classical period, *Wallenstein* (1799). His ideas about the nature of tragedy underwent fundamental changes. Gone is the villain, for Schiller realized that a story about an innocent man brought low by a blackguard tends to direct the audience's attention to the outward conflict. To focus attention on the inner struggle, he now prefers the aesthetic hero, the one who commits a crime, turns remorseful, and expiates it through self-punishment. Later still, as Schiller came to appreciate the role that chance and circumstance play in life, he added the concept of fatality and necessity. In the following pages, we shall see that *Wallenstein* displays many of these innovations.

I Wallenstein

Schiller conceived the idea for a drama about Albrecht von Wallenstein while doing the research for his tract *The History of the Thirty Years War* (1790–1792). Though he first mentions the theme's suitability for the stage in a letter to Körner dated 12 January 1791, he did not begin work on it until 1796. *Wallensteins Lager*, the first part of the trilogy, was completed just in time for Goethe to stage it at the gala reopening of the remodeled Weimar Theater on 12 October 1798. In January 1799 he finished *Die Piccolomini* and in early spring *Wallensteins Tod*. Thereupon, Goethe arranged for a sequential presentation of the completed work. The *Lager* on 15 April, *Die Piccolomini* on the seventeenth, and *Wallenstein's Tod* on the twentieth. The play was highly successful.

Schiller's trilogy dramatizes the last few days of the brief and brilliant career of Albrecht von Wallenstein, duke of Friedland, military genius, and commander in chief of all Catholic forces during the Thirty Years War (1618–1648). A sketch of his life shows what makes him suitable for dramatic treatment.

102

Wallenstein rose to prominence in 1626 when he offered the hardpressed Emperor Ferdinand II of Austria a fully equipped army of forty thousand men to fight the advancing Protestants. Since Ferdinand was on the verge of losing the war, the offer was more than welcome. For four years Wallenstein pursued the Protestants around central Europe winning spectacular victories. His successes, however, engendered jealousy in court circles. Eventually, influential power cliques pressured the emperor into rescinding Wallenstein's commission at the Diet of Regensburg in 1630. Stung, Wallenstein retreated to his estates in Bohemia to await, and to plan for, what he knew would be his inevitable recall.

In 1632 King Gustavus Adolphus of Sweden entered the war on the side of the Protestants. Also a commander of genius, he defeated one Catholic army after another. Soon he marched into Bavaria, crushed the armies there, and now prepared to invade Austria itself. Fear gripped the imperial court in Vienna. Ferdinand sent emissaries to Wallenstain with urgent pleas to resume command. But the duke refused until the emperor's situation became so desperate that he granted him powers which made him equal to the emperor in all but name.

No sooner had the duke resumed command than he drove the Saxon army out of Bohemia. Then, on 16 November 1632, he pitted his forces against Gustavus Adolphus in the awesome Battle of Lützen. The Swedes drove him from the field, but Gustavus was killed. Instead of pressing the advantage, Wallenstein withdrew to Pilsen, Bohemia, where he made camp for the winter. With court permission, he now opened peace negotiations with several Protestant states. At this point, the historical evidence blurs. The duke refused to sign any document in these negotiations. All the same, there is strong circumstantial evidence that he was concluding secret agreements with the enemy to promote personal ambitions. One report has it that he intended to merge his troops with the Swedes, march on Vienna, and crown himself emperor. Alarmed, the court launched an effort to remove the duke, who was murdered at the fortress town of Eger in 1634. Schiller's trilogy is structured loosely around the historical facts. His most notable additions are the characters Octavio Piccolomini and his son Max, the elevation of General Buttler to a major protagonist, the Max-Thekla episode, and the emphasis on Wallenstein's treasonous activities.

The situation at the beginning of the play indicates that Wallenstein has more or less decided to take the army over to the Swedes, force the emperor to sign a peace treaty, and to take the Bohemian crown as his part of the peace package. Over the years he has insured himself of the army's support by treating the common soldier well and by making military life more attractive than civilian life. He has gained the loyalty of the officer corps through special favors and by making their careers dependent on his own. If he falls, so do they all. Yet, as the curtain rises, Wallenstein has not decided on a definite course of action. He regards outright mutiny as a contingency plan to be invoked only as a last resort. The emperor, of course, believes that his commander is a threat to the throne. He therefore dispatches a special envoy, Questenberg, to the duke's camp with secret orders for Octavio Piccolomini, who is Wallenstein's best friend. Octavio had turned away from the duke when he realized the true nature of his friend's ambitions. Now he cooperates secretly with the court. The orders from Ferdinand appoint Octavio commander in chief above Wallenstein. Another document puts the duke under the imperial ban, a legal manoeuver which makes him wanted dead or alive. But Octavio is to invoke these powers only if the duke commits an overt act against the emperor. In the meantime, Octavio is to work behind the scenes to undermine the duke's influence. What he sees at Wallenstein's camp convinces Questenberg that he has arrived none too soon.

A   *The Elements of the Plot:* Wallensteins Lager

Wallensteins Lager is a vast panorama of Central Europe at the time of the Thirty Years War. Schiller here paints a vivid picture of the period. Besides introducing the historical background, which the audience needs to understand the action, he explains the political, social, economic, and military situation of the time. He even catches the spirit of the soldier and makes him into a collective protagonist who is rarely seen but whose presence is always felt. At the beginning of the piece, a group of soldiers are discussing why army life is the good life. The first Jäger contends that wartime army life is pleasurable because it liberates a man from humdrum reality, from the responsibility of home and family. The soldier does not have to worry about the past or the future. The sergeant agrees. Civilian life is dull. All it has to offer to a man is the prospect of sweating his life away at some tedious trade. Furthermore, a man is not chained to his station in life. He can rise to great heights if he has what it takes—like Buttler, who began as private and today salutes as general. It is war itself that all must thank, not politics and certainly not religion, which is laughed off the stage in the following scene.

A Capuchin friar harangues this group of soldiers. In ornate, baroque hyperbole he calls down the wrath of Heaven upon their sinful lives. Instead of making Europe safe for Catholicism, they lay about camp glutting their stomachs with food and drink, which they have taken by force from the emperor's subjects, the same subjects they are supposed to protect from plunder. Foul of mouth and black of soul, brawling, bragging, plundering scum, get up and spill the blood of Sweden's sons. The soldiers listen indifferently until he speaks ill of the duke, whereupon they drive him away with threats of violence. They have more important things on their mind than the cause, such as discussing the latest camp gossip.

Rumor has it that the emperor will detach eight regiments of the best troops from Wallenstein's forces to escort the Spanish infante through Germany to Holland. Everyone knows, though, that it is a ruse to weaken Wallenstein's power. And they do not like it. Their allegiance is to the duke, not to the emperor. So all the men agree among themselves to oppose any effort to disjoin them from their leader. *Wallensteins Lager* concludes as the troops gather round to sing of honor as the highest virtue and of the warrior's life as the best life.

B   *The Elements of the Plot:* Die Piccolomini

The action of *Die Piccolomini* begins at the moment when the last of Wallenstein's generals arrive at his headquarters in Pilsen. Officially, they have come to assist at informal meetings. But it is common knowledge that Wallenstein wants to test their loyalty. As Octavio says: "Wir sind berufen, uns ihm zu verkaufen, / Und weigern wir uns—Geisel ihm zu bleiben" ("We were called to sell ourselves to him, / And if we balk,—to be his hostages," I, 1).[1] In the first scenes, the confrontation between Questenberg and the generals Illo, Terzky, Buttler, and later Max Piccolomini demonstrates the officers' commitment to Wallenstein's cause. They tell Questenberg that they regard the imperial court as a clique of knavish courtiers who, spurred by jealous greed, intrigue shamelessly against their great leader. They will therefore resist any effort to dislodge him from command. Max is even more explicit. He will shed his blood, "Tropfenweis, eh dass / Ihr über seinen Fall frohlocken sollt!" ("by drops before / You shall exult above his fall," I, 4). Such open hostility alarms Questenberg; because if this is the general attitude, it is but a small matter to induce the army to outright mutiny. Octavio confirms in private that most of the army supports the duke. In the face of such loyalty, they must move carefully and in secret.

In act 2, Wallenstein himself appears on stage for the first time. After listening to his wife's account of what she has learned at the imperial court, he concludes that he has fallen from favor. He now decides that he has no choice but to move against the crown. Considering himself a victim of court intrigues, he proclaims: "O! sie zwingen mich, sie stossen / Gewaltsam, wider meinen Willen, mich hinein" ("Oh, they drive me to it, thrust me / By force against my will, right into it," II, 2). Enter Count Terzky, his brother-in-law and adviser, with the disturbing news that several generals have not come to the conference, sending transparent excuses. He tells the duke that if he continues to delay his move against Vienna other generals might leave the meeting. But Wallenstein hesitates, insisting that he does not desire rebellion. Yet his actions suggest otherwise. He orders Illo and Terzky to obtain for him at any cost a written declaration of support from the generals because such a document would be extremely useful in his bargaining with the Swedes. In order to get the document, Wallenstein resorts to trickery. First, he announces his intention to resign his command. This announcement frightens everyone whose career is tied to his. Then Terzky and Illo draw up a declaration of loyalty to Wallenstein for all the generals to sign. The first draft contains the key phrase "*So weit nämlich unser dem Kaiser geleisteter Eid es erlauben wird*" (". . . *insofar as the oath which we have sworn to the Emperor will permit,*" IV, 1). They circulate this version before dinner. Then after food and drink have dulled the wit, they substitute an exact copy which, however, omits the reference to their oath. The trick works and Wallenstein obtains his document.

After dinner Octavio meets privately with Max for the purpose of convincing him that Wallenstein plans treason (V, 1). He soon discovers to his annoyance that Max's faith in the duke is unshakeable. He disbelieves the charges of treason even when Octavio shows him classified documents. Not only that, he wants to know how his father could allow himself to be involved in such a sordid business. He tells Octavio that he will have nothing to do with this court-inspired spying mission. Everything has always been frank and open between him and the duke, whom he regards as his second father. Consequently, he will confront Wallenstein tomorrow with what he has learned today and demand an explanation.

Despite Max's forthright behavior, *Die Piccolomini* ends on a negative note. Deceit, plots, hatred, intrigues, jealousy, and self-interest reign. Momentous changes are in the offing, and everyone is taking sides.

C   *The Elements of the Plot: Wallenstein's Tod*

The opening scene depicts Wallenstein's belief in astrology. We learn that since his dismissal at Regensburg he has developed a strong belief in this occult science, which now rules his life. He judges a person's character by his horoscope, believes that dreams foretell the future, and never embarks on an important action without first consulting the stars. He has even engaged the services of a professional astrologer, Seni. In the first scene, Seni tells him that Venus, Jupiter, and Mars are in a favorable conjunction and that he can proceed with his plans assured of success. Yet the stars have not prepared Wallenstein for Terzky's sudden announcement that Sesina, his messenger to the Swedes, has been captured by imperial troops together with all the secret documents entrusted to him (I, 2). Staggered, the duke knows that he must act quickly, for the documents are highly incriminating. Before he takes the final step, he wants to see the Swedish envoy Wrangel, who has just arrived with a final proposal (III, 5).

Wrangel tells Wallenstein that if he is willing to cede to Sweden the capital city of Prague in a show of good faith, and prove to his satisfaction that he has the support of his commanders, they will give him the command of a Swedish army to march on Vienna. Wallenstein satisfies him with the loyalty oath which he had obtained under false pretenses. Still, Wallenstein dismisses him with a vague promise to consider the offer. He makes the decision only after Illo, Terzky, and especially Countess Terzky urge him to do so.

Act 2 commences with the confrontation between Wallenstein and Max. Max announces that he is willing to follow his friend anywhere and help him to fight any battle. But he is unwilling to break his oath to the Emperor by joining the enemy, for that is treason. When Max realizes that his efforts to dissuade Wallenstein are in vain, he walks out. Max is faced with a tragic dilemma. If he obeys the voice of duty and sides with the emperor, he loses his friend as well as the bride he hopes to gain. If he joins Wallenstein, he will be a traitor to God and country. He might even be required to fight against his own father.

While Max agonizes, Octavio intrigues to undermine the duke's support. He finds it easier than expected. Most of the generals reconfirm their loyalty to the emperor. Even General Buttler is reconverted after Octavio gives him written proof that Wallenstein is the real cause for his not receiving his promotion and patent of nobility (II, 6). When Octavio presents him with the imperial promotion, Buttler is all too glad to declare his allegiance to the emperor. Revenge in his heart, he requests that Octavio allow him to remain in Pilsen with Wallenstein. He tells Octavio that he cannot reveal his intentions, but that he should blindly trust him. Octavio makes a fatal error in judgment when he grants Buttler's wish; for driven by hatred and inspired by the thought of reward, the latter plans to murder Wallenstein. Thus Octavio shares responsibility for Wallenstein's death.

When act 3 begins, Wallenstein's rebellious intentions have become common knowledge. Large numbers of soldiers refuse to break their oath. All the commanders except Illo and Terzky desert. One catastrophe follows upon another. The report arrives that the garrison at Prague has refused the order to surrender and that all the regiments posted throughout Bohemia have reaffirmed their allegiance to the emperor. At this point a sudden change comes over Wallenstein. Decisive calm replaces the anxious indecision displayed until now. He appears suddenly as a different man. Despite his new determination to fight against overwhelming odds, his position deteriorates further.

Act 4 takes place the following afternoon at the fortress Eger on the frontier with Germany, where the remnants of the duke's forces are to join the Swedes on the next day. While Wallenstein inspects the city, Buttler makes preparations not only for his assassination but for the murder of all of the officers loyal to him. He will personally lead a team of assassins in a surprise attack upon the officer corps at the gala celebration that evening. After that, they will proceed to the duke's quarters and kill him. Later that same day the news of Max's death arrives (IV, 5). Unable to commit treason or to make war on Wallenstein, he has led his troops in a suicidal attack on the advancing Swedish army. After a brief struggle they are killed to the last man. Though grieved, Wallenstein regards the loss of Max as the price which Providence has extracted for the success of his rebellion.

With retardations and mounting suspense act 5 recounts the circumstances leading up to Wallenstein's death. Bad omens loom large but the duke disregards them all. A few minutes after he retires, Buttler and his men break into his quarters and kill him with their swords (V, 6). As the dead man is being carried out, Octavio arrives at the head of his army ready to take Wallenstein prisoner. Appalled at what has happened, he denounces Buttler's bloodthirsty deed as unnecessary and contrary to the emperor's wishes. Buttler shrugs his shoulders as he hurries off to Vienna to claim the reward, for he is convinced that everyone involved in the plot against the duke acted for motive of gain. His judgment seems to be justified, for as the curtain closes a messenger arrives with the news of Octavio's promotion to prince.

D   *Three Conflicting Forces*

During the first interview with Max, Wallenstein explains that they live in different worlds (*Tod*, II, 3). Max lives above in the bright realm of ideal values, where right behavior is its own reward and justification. Nature, on the other hand, fashioned Wallenstein of coarser stuff. His values center on this world, where the rewards are found in fame and fortune, power and position. He belongs to a world owned by the "spirits of darkness" who demand sacrifices before they yield up their possessions; and no one emerges morally pure from their service. This is the natural order of things to which the wise man accommodates himself. In this drama Wallenstein can be seen as a figure who represents the chaotic forces of nature, whereas Max reflects the concept of a priori morality. Juxtaposed to both is Octavio Piccolomini, the voice of tradition, duty, law and order. Flesh, spirit, and tradition; nature, morality, and custom are the main forces conflicting within this drama. If we now analyze these men in the light of Schiller's essays on aesthetics and poetry, we not only understand them better but we also appreciate how closely his philosophical speculations and his drama are related.

In Wallenstein's character Schiller emphasizes the negative qualities of the realist which he enumerates in his essay on poetry. We have learned that the realist is grounded in nature. He is attracted to the material and follows his inclinations without much thought. Motivated primarily by utilitarian considerations, he practices a form of situation ethics in which moral behavior conforms to whatever serves him best. This philosophy has served Wallenstein well because the world as he perceives it, and as it is described in this drama, is a moral wilderness little better than the physical state which Schiller describes in the *Twenty-Fourth Letter*. Here, men are driven by the ruthless pursuit of self-interest, motivated by jealousy, hatred, and the fear of one another's ambitions. Here, only the law of the jungle applies: the strong devour the weak. Here, the categorical imperative has been turned upside down to read: "Do it unto your neighbor before he does it unto you." As far as Wallenstein is concerned, everything is predetermined anyway. In his view, man has no control over his life. Predetermined necessity is the only force in the universe, and men are but cogs in a machine. It is folly to think otherwise; for as we speak of the laws of mathematics and of the laws of nature, so we also speak of the laws of human nature. Once we have plumbed a man's inmost soul, his every action becomes predictable. The deeds and thoughts of man well up from the inner world: "Sie sind notwendig, wie des Baumes Frucht, / Sie kann der Zufall gaukelnd nicht verwandeln" ("They are inevitable as fruit to trees, / And chance cannot juggle them in transformations," *Tod*, I, 4). Wallenstein's religion is a reflection of his worldview.

Indifferent to either Protestantism or Catholicism, astrology is Wallenstein's religion. Because the position of the stars represents for him the natural order of things, he, as an elemental force of nature, sees his life as an integral part of that great design. He finds meaning in astrology because, as a realist in the Schillerian sense, he sees chance, destiny, necessity, and character as different aspects of the same concept: "Es gibt keinen Zufall; / Und was uns blindes Ohngefähr nur dünkt, / Gerade das steigt aus den tiefsten Quellen" ("Chance / Does not exist. What seems blind chance to us, / Is just what rises from the deepest springs," *Tod*, II, 4).

Wallenstein's belief in astrology, necessity, and Fate contributes more than anything to his destruction. Soon after his dismissal at Regensburg he begins to organize his life around that occult science. He casts the horoscope of everyone around him, trusting the stars more than his own judgment. The result is that astrology clouds his natural talent for taking the measure of a man. He places, for example, implicit faith in Octavio simply because they were both born under the same configurations. He refuses to heed Illo's doubts concerning Octavio's trustworthiness because Illo's horoscope indicates that his judgment in such matters is destined to be faulty.

Astrology contributes to Wallenstein's destruction by also paralyzing his ability to make decisions. He hesitates to attack the emperor because he is waiting for Fate to reveal her design through what other men would call a chance event. This explains why he is relieved when the secret documents are captured and glad that the emperor: "kann mir nicht mehr trauen,—so kann ich auch / Nicht mehr zurück. Geschehe denn, .was muss. / Recht stets behält das Schicksal, denn das Herz / In uns ist sein gebietrischer Vollzieher" ("Can no longer trust me, / And I, on my side, can no more return. / Come then what must. Fate is forever in / The right, because the heart within us is / Its most obedient executive," *Tod,* I, 7). With a sense of relief he tells Max shortly thereafter that it is a blessing not to have a choice. When Max suggests that he leave his command voluntarily, he replies: "Doch hier ist keine Wahl. / Ich muss Gewalt ausüben oder leiden" ("But I have / No choice. I must use force or endure it," *Tod,* II, 2). Though he claims that he has no choice, we know that he does. He could give up his command and return to his estates. Yet he only has a choice in theory, for he relinquished free will when he declared for astrology.

The other factor contributing to Wallenstein's downfall is his woeful misjudgment of the common soldier. He knows that as long as the army follows him, he is invincible. Consequently, he expends considerable effort in maintaining that loyalty. He pays them well, he allows some of the regiments special privileges, and he makes life easy for his army. But he nevertheless makes a fundamental miscalculation in believing that its loyalty to him is absolute. Why does the army desert him? In the prologue to the drama Schiller says that:"Sein Lager nur erkläret sein Verbrechen" ("His camp alone will make his crime quite clear"). In *Wallenstein's Lager* we observe that the soldiers, like the duke himself, are indifferent to Catholicism or Protestantism. They regard themselves as a privileged elite spawned by fortune. They are proud of themselves and have a high concept of honor. The first cuirassier sums it up: "Der Soldat muss sich können fühlen. / Wer's nicht edel und nobel treibt,/ Lieber weit von dem Handwerk bleibt. / Soll ich frisch um mein Leben spielen, / Muss mir noch etwas gelten mehr" ("The soldier must feel a sense of his worth. / And one who does not act nobly would / Do well to steer clear of the trade for good./ If I am to risk my life on this earth/ There must be something more precious to vie for," *Lager,* II). He and his friends go on to identify honor as that precious something, in fact, their religion. This is a philosophy alien to Wallenstein who, as a realist, values the expedient over the honorable. Natural nobility escapes him: "Sein Charakter endlich ist niemals edel und darf es nie sein" ("His character in the final analysis is never noble and cannot be noble").[2] We may therefore say that the army deserts Wallenstein because when he asks his soldiers to break their word of honor to the emperor, it is the same as asking them to abandon their religion.

How then are we to judge Wallenstein? We might say that he is one of Schiller's ambiguous heroes whose character vacillates between the highest and the lowest in human nature. He can be strong, generous, tolerant, and fair-minded; but also an unscrupulous manipulator and master of dirty tricks. We can neither totally praise nor condemn him. Schiller tells us that Gordon, the commandant at Eger, represents the proper moral attitude toward the duke.[3] Throughout the final act, as Buttler makes the preparations for Wallenstein's death, Gordon counsels moderation and pleads with him not to do anything he might later regret. He urges Buttler to think of Wallenstein's good qualities while taking the bad in stride:

> O seiner Fehler nicht gedenket jetzt!
> An seine Grösse denkt, an seine Milde,
> An seines Herzens liebenswerte Züge,
> An alle Edeltaten seines Lebens,
> Und lasst sie in das aufgehobne Schwert
> Als Engel bittend, gnadeflehend fallen.

> O do not call his sins to memory now!
> Recall his greatness and his graciousness,
> Recall the winning features of his heart
> And all the noble actions of his life,
> And, like an angel pleading and imploring
> For mercy, let them check the upraised sword.

>   (IV, 8)

As a realist, Wallenstein follows the laws of necessity, but this does not exclude moments of nobility.

Opposite Wallenstein stands Max Piccolomini, who represents uncorrupted human nature. The circumstances of his life under Wallenstein's protection have made it possible for Max to develop without artifice. Consequently, there is an innocence and childlike simplicity about him which makes him a stranger to the corrupt society surrounding him. He is an anomaly, a genuine human being. In his daily activities he thinks and speaks the best about everyone, never pretends, always tells the truth, acts forthrightly, and remains true to himself throughout. Max can serve as a model for what Schiller in his essay *On Grace and Dignity*, called "a beautiful soul." Inner unity determines his orientation to the world. Unlike the realist, who looks to the outside world for direction, Max finds the answers within himself. His moral behavior is therefore spontaneous, devoid of artifice. He rejects participation in Octavio's intrigue because it is contrary to his nature. It does not matter that his father intrigues for higher purpose, because in Max's system the end never justifies the means. Schiller believed that deception not only defiles the noblest cause but also disrupts the inner equilibrium. Octavio's dissimulation has the same effect on the psyche as Wallenstein's treason.

Beautiful souls like Max can channel their strength into a sublime act in times of crisis. We recall that a sublime act requires that the desires of the heart be sacrificed to the demands of morality. In a *morally* sublime act the hero chooses to act according to principle even though he knows that his decision will bring him suffering or even death. Max is forced into such a situation when, through no fault of his own, he finds that he must choose between Wallenstein and his word of honor. He appears to face an insolvable dilemma. If he sides with duty, he will be forced to war against his second father and so experience the suffering that arises when we put duty before inclination. If he chooses Wallenstein and the heart, then he will experience the guilt that comes from violating a moral commitment. He solves the problem by leading his men in a suicidal attack on the Swedish army. His deed is morally sublime because he puts duty before inclination.

Contrasted to Wallenstein and Max is Octavio Piccolomini, a man of principle whose word, once given, can be relied on. He is never in any doubt as to where his allegiances lie. Consequently, when he discovers that Wallenstein plans to take the army over to the Swedes, he does not agonize over alternatives or experience an inner struggle. As he tells his son: "Hier gilt's, mein Sohn, dem Kaiser wohl zu dienen, / Das Herz mag dazu sprechen, was es will" ("The need here is, my son, to serve the Emperor. / To that the heart may say what it may say," (*Picc.*, V, 1). This is the premise for his moral activity—not revenge, hatred, or material gain. Despite Max's accusations that his father profits from his friend's fall, and despite his promotion to the rank of prince, there is no evidence in the drama to suggest that Octavio is a political opportunist or that he acts from motive of gain. He is certainly not in the same category with the profiteering commanders Buttler, Illo, Terzky, and Isolan. To pursue reward is not the same as expecting to be rewarded for services rendered. If wealth and power were Octavio's aim, he stands to gain more by serving Wallenstein, who had already promised him two duchies as his part of the peace package. From the evidence it is clear that his ambitions do not extend beyond loyalty to the emperor, the symbol of tradition, law, and order.

The fate of Wallenstein, Max, and Octavio brings up another question. Since the trilogy is about history in the making, can it be regarded as Schiller's statement about the historical process? Since the author was also a professional historian, such a possibility seems likely. Although he delighted in dissecting his own plays, he never indicated whether he meant this drama as an illustration of his philosophy of history. Nevertheless, if we look at the piece as a formulation of his historical theories, we see that it conforms to his ideas expressed in the essay on aesthetics.

The three forces at work in the historical process and in this drama are (1) the determining, but often fickle or cruel forces of nature as represented by Wallenstein, (2) morality as represented by Max, and (3) tradition, custom, law, and order as represented by Octavio and the court. Morality as a guiding force is discounted when Max's system proves unable to ensure his survival. Natural, or by extension, divine intention is discounted when Wallenstein is murdered. That leaves tradition and custom as the guiding force. This conclusion accords with Schiller's ideas about social evolution. In the *Fifth Letter* he discusses revolution as a method of social improvement and concludes that it brings out the worst in man. Tradition, growth, maturation, and aesthetic education pave the way to progress. In dramatizing Wallenstein's and Max's destruction, he discounts either nature or morality as playing the decisive role in the historical process.

II   Maria Stuart

Schiller completed *Wallenstein* in March 1799. By the end of April he was reading a history of Elizabethan England and studying the life and trial of Mary Stuart, Queen of Scots, who is the subject of his next drama. He began writing in June, and by September he had finished acts 1 and 2 and part of act 3. His wife's illness in the autumn, the family's removal to Weimar in December, and an illness of his own delayed the project until May of 1800, when he retired to the estate of a friend, where he finished the drama. The play met with resounding success at its first performance on 14 June.

The story of Mary Stuart ranks among history's most famous tales.

Since the historical facts form the background of the play, a brief summary of her life is called for. Mary was the granddaughter of Henry VII Tudor and the first born of James V Stuart of Scotland. She was therefore in the line of succession to two kingdoms. Related on her mother's side to the powerful dukes and cardinals of Guise in France, Mary was sent abroad at the age of six to be raised at the French court. In 1558, at age sixteen, she married the Dauphin Francis. In the marriage procession she displayed the royal emblems of France, England, and Scotland as if she were already queen in all three countries. This was Catholic Europe's spectacular way of challenging the legitimacy of Protestant Elizabeth, who had ascended the English throne that same year. For under Catholic law Elizabeth was merely the bastard offspring of Henry VIII and Anne Boleyn. But under Protestant law, which permits divorce, Elizabeth was legitimate and therefore legally queen. Eventually England, France, and Scotland sought to draft a treaty in which Mary would renounce her claims to England for as long as Elizabeth lived. Her refusal to sign marks the beginning of the long feud between Mary and Elizabeth.

In 1559 the French king was killed in a jousting match, bringing Francis and Mary to the throne. Francis died the next year, and Charles IX became king, which meant that the queen mother, Catherine de Medici, became the power behind the throne. A Machiavellian woman, she soon had sole authority in France. At about this time news arrived from Scotland that, owing to the death of Mary's mother, she was now queen of Scotland. Since Mary's position at the French court had become intolerable, she returned home.

The new queen of Scotland was extremely popular at first. The country was captivated by her looks and by her personality. Besides, she took her duties seriously and tried to rule effectively. She was a diplomat as well. As a conciliatory gesture she asked Elizabeth's advice in choosing a suitable husband. Elizabeth's first choice was her own lover Lord Leicester. This proved to be an unwise choice since he and Mary disliked each other instantly. Elizabeth then sent the dashing Lord Darnley. To the surprise of everyone Mary fell passionately in love with him, and they were soon married. Their child was to become the future James I of England.

Mary's passion for her husband cooled when shortly after the marriage Darnley revealed his true character. Though only the royal consort, he played king. Besides attempting to eclipse Mary, he was insanely jealous of her. Believing gossip that his wife had taken the court singer Rizzio as lover, he burst into her rooms one evening with several companions and murdered the singer before her eyes. Mary's dislike now turned into open hatred. She conspired secretly with her real lover James Hepburn, earl of Bothwell, to murder Darnley. On 9 February 1567 Bothwell blew up the house where Darnley was staying. Not a victim of the blast, Darnley was found strangled to death in a nearby garden. Since Mary was elsewhere at the time of the explosion, and since it was common knowledge that she hated her husband, the public concluded her direct involvement. When Mary married his murderer three months later, a rage of indignation swept the country. Soon a group of Protestant noblemen gathered an army to force her abdication.

Her armies destroyed, Mary fled to England and sought asylum with Elizabeth. The English queen was not overjoyed at the prospect because she saw Mary as a threat since her claim to the English throne was supported by Europe's Catholic monarchs. So Elizabeth decided to detain her temporarily. Temporary detainment soon became permanent imprisonment. In the following years, there were unsuccessful plots and conspiracies to free the Scottish queen. After the famous Babington attempt Elizabeth appointed a commission to try Mary on fabricated charges of treason. Her guilt was proved by expertly forged documents called "The Casket Letters." She was beheaded at Fotheringhay Castle on 8 February 1587.

Schiller, as was his custom, changes some facts of Mary Stuart's life for dramatic purposes. He moves the date of execution from 8 to 12 February and opens the action on the ninth, which is the anniversary of Lord Darnley's death. Since Mary also hears that the commission has condemned her to death, Schiller establishes a dramatic link between the crime and the punishment. Schiller also invents the fanatical Mortimer, the love between Lord Leicester and Mary, and the meeting of the queens in act 3. Finally, he relocates Fotheringhay Castle, Mary's prison, nearer London.

A   The Elements of the Plot

The first scenes of act 1 portray the circumstances of Mary's imprisonment and the state of her mind. We learn that she has been deprived of all her attendants except for Jane Kennedy. She is forced to live in Spartan simplicity. She may neither receive visitors nor communicate with the outside world. And she lacks the respect of her jailor, Sir Amias Paulet, who regards her as a dangerous, scheming woman who must be watched carefully. When Mary makes her first appearance, the circumstances of her life manifest themselves in three main emotions. She is a woman embittered by the deprivations and indignities which she has suffered. Naturally, she blames Elizabeth for her misery. She nourishes a deep hatred for the English queen and lives her days dreaming of revenge. Second, she tells Kennedy that her conscience aches because of her involvement in her husband's death. Third, she waits anxiously for the verdict of the royal commission which has just tried her for treason. Thus hatred, remorse, and anxiety are the forces dominating Mary's mind.

Just at the point where Mary Stuart's fortunes appear at an ebb, hope arrives from an unexpected quarter. Sir Paulet's nephew, Mortimer, visits her secretly to tell a remarkable tale. During a recent sojourn in France and in Italy, he renounced his Protestant faith and became an ardent Catholic. With the blessing, training, and financial assistance of Mary's relatives, he has returned to England at the head of a conspiracy to free her by force. Mary, of course, is delighted at the prospect. Convinced of his sincerity, she asks him to include Lord Leicester in his plans. She sends Mortimer to Leicester with a letter containing her picture as proof that he can be trusted. In the letter she promises herself to Leicester as prize if only he will help her escape. During the conversation Mary fails to notice Mortimer's veiled declaration of love.

In act 2, the action switches to the royal court at Westminster where Elizabeth sits in counsel with her advisers discussing the wisdom of sending Mary to the block. Burleigh, who always has the best interests of the state at heart, speaks for her immediate execution for reasons of national security. Leicester, who always has his own best interests at heart, argues for postponement. Shrewsbury, who considers such an execution not only immoral but also illegal, speaks for clemency. Elizabeth hesitates to order a public execution for she wants to avoid all semblance of personal involvement. She knows that such a deed would incur the wrath of the continental powers. She would prefer to dispose of Mary in some less dramatic fashion, such as that which, secretly and unknown to others, she suggests to Mortimer in the following scene.

Mortimer has come to court with Sir Paulet to deliver the papers which a search of Mary's apartment has produced. One of the documents is a letter from Mary requesting an interview with Elizabeth. There ensues a hot debate as to the wisdom of granting the request. Burleigh points out that Elizabeth must not do so because a pardon always attends the royal presence. Elizabeth promises to consider the arguments and dismisses court, except for Mortimer. She has a plan to ask Mortimer to do away with Mary quietly. That way she will be able to avoid signing the warrant. Mortimer accepts the commission for two reasons. He wants to prevent her from hiring other assassins and to gain time to assemble his own confederates.

After the interview with Elizabeth, Mortimer has the opportunity to give Lord Leicester Mary's letter. We learn that his lordship plays a double role at court. He pretends devotion to Elizabeth while negotiating secretly with Mary, primarily because now that Eliza-beth has decided to marry the Duc d'Anjou he will lose his favored position at court. Still, Leicester will have nothing to do with Mortimer's plan to free her by force, for he is not a courageous man. Instead, he will persuade Elizabeth to see Mary so as to tie her hands until means can be found to liberate the prisoner. Mortimer now regards his lordship as a weakling beneath contempt.

Act 3 describes the meeting between the queens. Although prearranged, it is made to appear a coincidence. Mary is allowed to walk outside in the park where Elizabeth will chance to rest from the exertions of the royal hunt. Although the interview takes Mary completely by surprise, she manages to get control of her emotions. At first all goes well. But when Elizabeth provokes Mary with offensive references to her numerous love affairs, Mary's hatred, which has been smoldering beneath the surface, flames up violently. She scorches Elizabeth with the greatest of insults: "Der Thron von England ist durch einen Bastard / Entweiht" ("The throne of England is profaned by a bastard").[4] Elizabeth leaves in a fury, and Mary has destroyed whatever chance she may have had for a pardon.

Mary's performance bewitches Mortimer, who has been watching from a distance. He rushes up in violent agitation to reveal his love for her. His effusions are interrupted by the sudden news that one of the conspirators, a religious zealot, has attempted to assassinate the English queen on the way back to London. The conspiracy is broken, and all the confederates are fleeing for their lives. Act 3 ends in confusion.

Act 4 takes place at Westminster later that day. It dramatizes the events leading up to the signing of Mary's death warrant. In a room of the palace, Lord Leicester sickens in fear when Mortimer tells him that a half-written letter from Mary to him speaking of their agreement has fallen into Burleigh's hands, which means that he has given it to Elizabeth, which in turn means that Leicester's life is in danger. Desperate to save himself, he hits upon a bold plan. He calls the guards and orders them to arrest Mortimer for treason. Seeing himself betrayed, Mortimer takes his own life cursing Elizabeth. Leicester is saved. With the guard as witness he proceeds to the royal chambers, where he gives the greatest performance of his career. He succeeds in completely exonerating himself. He even calls for Mary's immediate execution. He has to pay for his victory, though; for later he is placed in charge of the execution. After listening once more to Shrewsbury protesting the execution, Elizabeth withdraws with the unsigned warrant.

Following a highly rational monologue, Elizabeth signs the document in the firm conviction that, all things considered, she acts in England's best interests. Still wishing to avoid personal responsibility for her rival's death, she gives the warrant to her secretary Davison without telling him exactly how to proceed with it. Her ambiguity in this matter is heavily emphasized. Later, as Davison stands alone wondering what to do, Burleigh appears, snatches it from his hands, and leaves with Leicester for Fotheringhay.

Act 5 takes place first at Fotheringhay Castle and later at Westminster. Mary's reaction to her impending death is highly important because it marks the onset of her spiritual renewal. When she appears on stage, we see that a great change has occurred. Serene and calm, she has reconciled herself to her fate. She has forgotten about her hatred and her worldly aims. Her thoughts are not turned inward in self-pity but outward to the welfare of her friends. She counters their anguish with a cheerful mood. It is not her hour of death she says, but her hour of triumph. For she goes to her death in the conviction that this unjust political execution for a crime of which she is innocent is God's way of allowing her to atone for Darnley's death—a crime of which she is guilty. Just as she is about to follow Burleigh to the room directly below, where the headsman waits, she catches sight of Leicester, who has been standing off to one side, eyes downcast. She tells him that she forgives him and wishes him well. The room empties and Leicester stands alone.

Schiller describes the execution through Leicester, who can hear the proceedings through the floor. When the ax falls, Leicester faints. He arises a new man. Soon thereafter he sails for France abandoning court life. He too has experienced a renewal.

While these events are taking place, Elizabeth waits anxiously at

Westminster. She has been so successful at avoiding personal involvement that she does not know what is happening. When Burleigh finally enters to announce Mary's death, she pretends to have been misunderstood, that the Scottish queen's death was not her intention—spoken or implied. Later she publishes this position throughout Europe. To prove her sincerity, she banishes Burleigh and orders Davison to the Tower. Talbot, disgusted at her behavior, leaves her forever. As the curtain falls, Elizabeth stands alone.

B *Crime and Punishment*

Perhaps the most salient feature of the play is the dramatization of Mary's and Lord Leicester's moral turpitude and subsequent spiritual renewal. The part of the drama dealing with this aspect follows the four stages leading to aesthetic sublimity discussed in chapter 1: crime, guilt, and punishment followed by renewal.

Maria Stuart is Schiller's only play in which the crime takes place before the action begins. This tells us that his main interest centers on working out the effect of the crime on the mind of the perpetrator and those around her. Besides Mary, Leicester is the one most affected by the chain of events. To bring out the magnitude of the changes wrought in Mary's and Leicester's character, the drama first points to the destructive side of their lives. In Mary's case, we see her in the beginning as a woman of violent passions who flaunts tradition, custom, and morality in her thoughtless pursuit of self-gratification. She satisfies her inclinations at any price. As we have learned, she stops at nothing until at last, impelled by hatred mingled with erotic passion, she conspires with Bothwell to kill her husband. When she marries the murderer, her people finally drive her from the throne.

The crimes committed, Mary enters the second stage, that of the experience of guilt. We observe that her feelings of remorse are as intense as her passions. Mary's first efforts to expiate her guilt through self-punishment fail to ease her sufferings because the pain endured does not equal the crime in magnitude. A murder cannot be atoned by fasting and prayer, as she knows herself: "Und er wird nimmer Friede mit mir machen, / Bis meines Unglücks Mass erfüllet ist" ("He will never make his peace with me / Until misfortune's measure has been filled / For me," I, 4). Nevertheless, the very fact that she feels remorseful and accepts the responsibility for her actions shows that her regeneration is already underway when the dramatic action begins. But she still has a long way to go.

She has yet to liberate herself from her hatred of Elizabeth. Hatred wins a spectacular victory over her in the interview with Elizabeth, where it transforms her temporarily. Mary presents a shocking spectacle, gloating as she hurls insults and savors victory. In this scene darkness celebrates the victory over light and hatred becomes the life force.

The announcement of Mary's impending execution triggers the victory over her hatred. Schiller does not dramatize the events of the transformation itself; rather, he stages the results through a change in the way Mary moves about. We recall from his essay on sublimity that the object of tragedy is to show the mind's ability to transcend misfortune. Since freedom is a formless quality, its presence is noticed only by its effects on physical behavior. In act 5, Mary's body language shows what freedom looks like. To make the transformation vivid, Schiller first portrays the look of emotional servitude. When the third act closes, we see Mary overwrought and ravaged by her worst qualities. When she reappears in the fifth act, she is just the opposite. The stage directions specify composure and serenity. She is cheerful. She acts like someone who has been relieved of a great burden. It is her hour of triumph; for having won the victory over her hatred, she can forgive Leicester and Elizabeth for their actions against her. More important, by accepting the political execution as an opportunity to expiate her great guilt, she turns Leicester's and Elizabeth's self-interested manipulations into the means of her spiritual renewal—and that is the ultimate victory.

Like Mary, Lord Leicester also undergoes a spiritual renewal. When we first meet him, we see that he, like Mary, is dedicated to the ruthless pursuit of self-interest. Thoroughly materialistic and morally shallow he will do anything to achieve his aims. His value system is particularly evident in his first encounter with Mortimer, where, in a paroxysm of self-pity, he complains about how for ten years he has catered to Elizabeth's whims, sacrificed his pride upon the altar of her vanity, endured humiliation, and sold his self-respect. Now that the reward is within his grasp, she will marry a Frenchman. Destiny has cruelly denied him his rightful prize. He has invested the best years of his life for nothing. Casting about for a way to restore his fortunes, he opens secret negotiations with Mary without any moral qualms. He will free her if she will make him the royal consort. Leicester acts ruthlessly until he confronts Mary face to face in act 5. Her sublime transfiguration shatters his resolve and precipitates a series of insights about himself which culminate in his spiritual renewal. When he finally realizes how greed and lure of fame have transformed him into a moral Quasimodo, he loses his sense of self-worth. He feels remorse for the first time.

Schiller stages Leicester's death and transfiguration in the scene where he listens to the sounds of the execution. At first he tries to play his role to the end and witness the execution. Yet when he attempts to force himself, something inside of him rebels. Once he gathers up all his strength and makes it halfway to the stairs before a great pain stops him cold: "Umsonst! Umsonst! Mich fasst der Hölle Grauen, / Ich kann, ich kann das Schreckliche nicht schauen" ("In vain! In vain! Hell's anguish seizes me! I cannot, cannot force myself to see the ghastly sight!" V, 10). When he wants to rush out of the room but finds the doors locked, he is gripped by terror—for he is experiencing his own execution. When the ax falls in the room below, it symbolically kills the old Leicester. When he arises from his faint he is a different man. Since he sails for France and thus turns his back on the rewards awaiting him at Westminster, we conclude that this is not only a form of voluntary punishment to expiate guilt but also a comment upon the insights gained. In a way he is like the student of the ballad *Das Verschleierte Bild zu Sais* who learns that if we obtain the things we want in life through wrongdoing, we will find no pleasure in them.

C   *Fanaticism*

Mortimer could be left out altogether without altering the outcome of the drama—which does not diminish his importance, however. Mortimer serves, first of all, to illuminate specific qualities of the various protagonists. Mary's effect on him, for example, illustrates the intoxicating impact that her magnetism is said to have exerted upon men. In his desire to possess her, Mortimer is even willing to murder his uncle and plunge England into civil war. In fact, he seems to bring out the worst in everyone. Elizabeth bargains with him to kill Mary secretly, and Leicester reaches the nadir of his career when he denounces him to save himself. Mortimer has a negative influence on events and people because he is a fanatic.

Mortimer can be regarded as an example of the fanatic whom Schiller describes in his essay on human types, where he says that he represents the caricature, or perverted extreme, of the idealist. We recall from chapter 1 that the idealist frees himself from nature because he seeks a separate, more universal reality beyond the here and now. Yet he is not free of restraint in his actions because he subordinates himself to moral principles of his own creation. As he ascends to greater heights in his quest, he arouses in us a lofty conception of the human potential. The fanatic, by contrast, illustrates the depths into which it is possible to sink. He is also free of nature, but he has not inaugurated a set of moral principles. His divorce from nature has but one aim: "Um dem Eigensinne der Begierden und den Launen der Einbildungskraft desto ungebundner nachgeben zu können" ("To better indulge the wantonness of his desires and the whims of his imagination").[5] The result of liberation from any governing principle whatsoever is illustrated from yet another angle when Mortimer and his confederates receive the church's remission not only of their past crimes but also of any which they may commit in the future. Thus released from all moral and religious constraint, they may commit the most appalling acts with impunity. They do not stand above the law, but are lawless. Even the instinct of self-preservation is powerless to prevent Mortimer from destroying himself.

D *Elizabeth*

The queen of England is Mary's opposite in every way. Whereas Mary is rooted in the world of sense, Elizabeth is grounded in reason. She stands for civilization, order, self-discipline. Unlike Mary, she undergoes no change of character during the drama; as she is in the beginning, so she is at the end. She lives and thrives in a world of power politics, where the end justifies the means. Whereas Mary is known for her unrestrained self-indulgence, Elizabeth subordinates her personal feelings and her life to the welfare of the state. England's good underlies even her more dubious actions, as the following discussion shows.

When Elizabeth is on stage for the first time in the second act, she is negotiating a nonaggression pact with France which she hopes to seal with a marriage to the Duc d'Anjou. By her own admission, she is emotionally uninvolved with him. In fact, if it were a matter of personal preference, she would remain single or marry Leicester. Even so, she is prepared to sacrifice her own wishes to England's security. Again in the following scene, where she and her advisers consider Mary's fate, she appears coldly practical. This is not to say that Elizabeth is devoid of human emotion; when she reads Mary's letter she weeps tears of compassion. It means only that she does not allow feeling to influence her judgment in matters of state, or her conscience either for that matter. She conspires with Mortimer and finally signs the order of execution without ever deliberating upon the moral quality of her actions. For her, Mary's death is a matter of political expediency.

Elizabeth's deception concerning Mary's death illuminates her political skills most effectively. First, she engages Mortimer to dispose of Mary in some undramatic fashion. This way she avoids signing the order of execution. Next, she tricks Lord Leicester into persuading her to grant a semiofficial interview with Mary—not for the purpose of flattering her female ego, it must be stressed, but because a pardon always attends the royal presence. She is fully aware that seeing Mary will be interpreted both at home and abroad as a sign that she intends to change the sentence. Then when Mary dies in Mortimer's custody, her hands will be clean. Or if Mortimer is unsuccessful, she can give the signed warrant to Davison and claim innocence later. She can say that Mary's execution was a mistake. Others acted without authorization. Mary's death was not her wish at all. Why, did she not recently grant her adversary an interview in a show of good faith? Did she not banish Burleigh and send Davison to the Tower?

We should not conclude our discussion of the drama without calling attention to its symmetrical structure. The action is divided equally between Mary and Elizabeth. Act 1 and most of act 5 take place at Fotheringhay. Acts 2 and 4 are devoted to Elizabeth, and act 3 brings the queens together. Mary lives in unembellished simplicity, Elizabeth in the opulence of Westminster. Each queen has an admirer who reflects her character. As Mortimer's rash, hot-blooded nature is the extreme of Mary's personality, so Leicester's unscrupulous intrigues mirror Elizabeth's machinations. Whereas both Mortimer and Mary die, Leicester and Elizabeth live—but in loneliness. The final moments of Mary's life are spent surrounded by the love of her friends while she experiences the intense joy of spiritual renewal and goes to her death transfigured. Elizabeth, though victorious, stands alone at the end, abandoned by Leicester, condemned by Shrewsbury, and wondering: "Was zittr' ich? Was ergreift mich diese Angst?" ("Why am I trembling? Why does terror seize me?" V, 12).

III   Die Jungfrau von Orleans

Two weeks after *Maria Stuart* premiered on 1 July 1800, Schiller began work on *Die Jungfrau von Orleans* [The Maid of Orleans]. He worked on the project leisurely until February 1801, when he read the finished parts to Goethe, whom he wanted to consult about the ending he had in mind. Goethe liked what he heard and gave him all the encouragement he needed. Schiller wrote steadily until he completed the drama on 16 April. It played successfully first in Leipzig, then in Berlin, and finally in Weimar on 23 April 1803. Several times Schiller enjoyed the success in person: when he attended a performance in Leipzig, he was treated to a standing ovation. He also saw a performance in Berlin, where a theatrical festival had been organized in honor of his visit there. For two generations thereafter the drama was part of the repertory of virtually every German theater.

The historical events behind the action on the stage concern the most eventful phase of the Hundred Years Wars (1346–1453). The war was begun by King Edward III of England who, on the death of King Charles IV of France, demanded the French throne. He justified his claim through his mother, who was the sister of Charles. But since in France the Salic Law prohibits accession to the throne through the female line, the French ignored his claim. The struggle between England and France far outlasted the two monarchs. After several decades of indecisive conflict the war lapsed into a stalemate. Then in 1415 Henry V of England launched a new campaign, winning a major victory at Agincourt. Within five years vast portions of what is now modern France were in his hands. Beaten, Charles VI signed the Treaty of Troyes (1420) which guaranteed Henry's succession to the French throne on the death of Charles. In 1422 both kings died, whereupon France declared the treaty void. The duke of Bedford, however, reopened the war in the name of the child king, Henry VI. The Burgundians, who were France's most powerful allies, sided with the English to revenge themselves on the Dauphin—the French crown prince—who had murdered their duke. Within six years the combined forces of England and Burgundy had conquered Paris and all of France down to the river Loire. In 1428 they laid siege to Orleans. Just as the French were on the verge of capitulation, a seventeen-year-old peasant girl from the village Domremy in eastern France arrived at the dauphin's court at Chinon. She related a remarkable story of how she was in communion with heavenly spirits who told her that God had chosen her to liberate France and crown the Dauphin King Charles VII at the cathedral at Rheims. She met with many objections, but finally her belief in her divine mission persuaded her hearers that she was sent by God. Joan put on a soldier's uniform and rode at the head of her troops. Impressed and inspired by her faith, the fainthearted French took courage.

On 29 April 1429, under Joan's command, the French drove the English from Orleans. In June she won a major victory at Patay. Then she liberated Rheims, where she attended the coronation. In September she led the French in an unsuccessful attack on occupied Paris, where she received her first wound. The mystique of her invincibility destroyed, her campaign lost momentum. Charles and many others at court began to doubt the divine nature of her mission. Finally, the Burgundians captured her and sold her to the English, who brought her to trial before an ecclesiastical- court, to be tried as a witch. She was condemned to death. Two years after the relief of Orleans she was burned at the stake in Rouen. She was canonized in 1920. After her death the English won no more victories. By 1453 all the English possessions except Calais were in the hands of the French king.

Though Schiller uses the historical facts as the frame for the first four acts, he changes the ending and makes Joan die on the field of battle. The author felt perfectly justified in his alterations because poetry is not history. Nor should it be in the service of history, which would be the case if the dramatist described everything exactly as it happened. When the attention switches from aesthetic appreciation to the facts, the piece ceases to be art. If it is to be judged fairly, the play should be viewed within its own context and judged according to aesthetic principles.

A   The Elements of the Plot

The drama begins with the prologue. In it, we are transported to the village of Domremy to observe the circumstances of Joan's life before she takes up her mission. Through the words of her father, Thibaut d' Arc, and her suitor, Raimond, we learn that Joan is a solitary person who likes nothing better than tending her father's sheep high up in the mountains. Her favorite spot is a small roadside chapel near an ancient oak known locally as the Druid Tree. A superstitious man, Thibaut believes the legend that since olden times an evil spirit dwells beneath the tree. He fears that it has possessed his daughter, which accounts for her strange behavior. Raimond agrees that she exhibits the manner of someone whose mind dwells in other places. But that is because she is in communion with blessed spirits. Later we learn from Joan that on the last three nights the Virgin Mary appeared to her in a vision and told her to put on armor, go to the Dauphin's court, and tell him that God has chosen her to drive the English from Orleans, liberate the ancient city of Rheims, and crown him king there. In all of this, God will guide her. There is, however, one condition: for the duration of her mission she must not love any man: "Nicht Männerliebe darf dein Herz berühren / Mit sünd'gen Flammen eitler Erdenlust" ("With man's love thou shalt never be embraced / Nor passion's sinful flame thy heart invest").[6]

The events of act 1 are close to fact. Joan arrives at Chinon as France hovers on the brink of final defeat. She convinces the astonished court of her divine mission, receives command of the army, and leaves for Orleans. Charles sends with her his highest officers, Dunois and La Hire.

Act 2 takes place much later on the field of battle. Intoxicated by the charismatic maiden, the French forces at Orleans fall upon the hapless besiegers. Seized by panic, the enemy flees into the countryside with Joan's victorious legions in hot pursuit. Now we see her in action. She overtakes an Englishman, Montgomery, who is fleeing for his life. He throws down his weapons, falls on his knees, and begs for mercy. He appeals to her compassion and to her woman's heart. But she tells him that she is not subject to human emotion. It is her obligation to kill whomever the divine hand guides into her path. She forces him to fight her and skillfully strikes him dead. Joan's skill with weapons matches her craft with words. In the following scene she meets the duke of Burgundy, melts his heart, and wins him over to France. Later, when the dauphin wants to find her a suitable mate as reward for her efforts, she replies that though she feels honored, the prospect revolts her; for to carry a man's image in her heart would profane her holy mission. The dauphin and all the members of the court disagree. Only the announcement of an English counterattack prevents the exchange from growing hostile.

Upon her return to the battlefield Joan has a remarkable experience. She notices a knight of high rank clad all in black. Pursuing him, he adroitly maneuvers her to the battle's edge, where he turns to await her approach. He pronounces a dire warning: Rheims will fall and there she will witness the coronation: "Gehe / In keinen Kampf mehr. Höre meine Warnung!" ("Enter no more battles. Heed my warning!"). Joan, however, does not take heed and, as she draws back her sword to kill him, he immobilizes her with the touch of his hand, then sinks into the earth.

No sooner has the apparition vanished than the English commander, Lionel, appears. She attacks him despite the warning. As
they fight, she tears the helmet off his head, looks into his face, and,
to her shock and dismay, feels "*sünd'gen Flammen eitler Erdenlust*". So smitten, she chooses to spare his life. When she realizes
what has happened, she is stricken with remorse. By falling in love,
she has betrayed her mission. To make matters worse, Lionel returns
her love. When she refuses to go with him to the English camp, he
wrestles away her sword to guarantee another meeting. The loss of
her sword symbolizes the loss of her special powers and her fall from
grace.

In act 4 a great change has come over Joan. She is no longer the
warrior maiden inspired by divine self assurance. Gloomy and
despondent, she sits alone reflecting on her love and on her fall. She
has absolutely no desire to participate in the coronation parade, and
does so only because her friends insist. During the procession she
walks with unsure step, betraying her inner turmoil.

Joan's opportunity to regain what she lost comes right after the
coronation. Her father has come to Rheims because he is still
laboring under the misapprehension that his daughter is under the
spell of the spirit dwelling beneath the Druid Tree. He confronts
her in the middle of the street and publicly denounces her as a
brazen, cheating, serving girl in league with dread spirits. He
challenges her to prove him a liar by swearing before God that she
is saintly and pure. When she makes no reply even King Charles
assumes her guilt. Unmindful of all that Joan has done, he banishes
her from his kingdom. Joan submits to the unjust punishment
willingly. Unknown to others, she is using the punishment to expiate
her real guilt. As the curtain falls on the fourth act, Raimond
appears and leads her away.

For three days, Joan and Raimond wander alone through the
Ardennes Forest in a raging storm. Eventually an English column
appears and takes her captive. Soon imprisoned in a castle under
heavy guard, she receives a visit from Lionel, who pleads with her
to marry him. She refuses because she has overcome her love for
him. Having undergone a change of heart, Charles attacks the castle
to free the maiden. At first the battle rages back and forth
indecisively. Then the English gain the upper hand. Just as the
French army is on the verge of collapse, Joan addresses a frantic
prayer of help to God. Suddenly reendowed with her old power, she

breaks asunder her chains, overpowers a nearby guard, and with his sword rushes into the thick of battle, where her inspired example turns defeat into victory. Yet the victors are in anguish for she is mortally wounded. In her dying speech we see her once again in unity with the spiritual realm. At the end of the drama, the commanders honor her by covering her body with their banners.

B   *Two Kinds of Sublimity*

Unlike *Maria Stuart*, which has two major characters as well as an important supporting cast, *Die Jungfrau von Orleans* focuses heavily on the heroine. Though colorfully drawn, the other main characters suffer from a lack of development. The dramatic action revolves about the events of Joan's fall and renewal. Unlike Mary, Joan displays moral as well as aesthetic sublimity. The following discussion concentrates on her fall and regeneration.

The meaning of what happens to Joan is to be found in her contract with God. The stipulation that she resist earthly love is another way of saying that she must maintain herself in a state of sublimity by her will. Schiller says that a person is *morally* sublime if he resists an impulse to transgress a moral law. Whatever pain is endured in the process is therefore derived from an act of will. Joan's behavior through the first three acts is morally sublime because she resists any intrusions from her heart that would deflect her from her purpose. Though Raimond, Dunois, and La Hire love her, she is emotionally indifferent to them. Consequently, she appears strange, otherwordly to her friends at home and cold to the royal court. Her feeling always in bondage to will, Joan's humanity remains hidden. She listens in hostile incomprehension to talk of love and marriage. As she tells Montgomery before executing him, her mission is everything. Money and property as well as compassion and pity are alien deities for which she has no use. This is not to say that Joan cannot feel. Staring at the dead Montgomery, she marvels that though a part of her melts with compassion for the men she slays, and though she shivers at the sight of swords, when circumstances so require she is imbued with the power to do what is necessary.

Although Joan overcomes her compassion for Montgomery, she falls victim to her love for Lionel. Her transgression in Lionel's case is not so much that she loves him but that she is unable to subordinate the emotion to her mission. Here we must emphasize that Schiller is not presenting love as a negative quality. There is no evidence that he had a low opinion of this emotion. Love is at fault only if it prevents us from doing what is right. In Joan's case, right behavior means fidelity to the requirements of her mission, about which she is quite well informed. Not only is she forbidden to love, she is obligated to kill anyone whom the divine hand places in her path. Within the framework of her contract, she is morally obligated to kill Lionel. Yet she chooses to spare his life. At that moment her divine powers vanish and she becomes human.

The transition from sublimity to humanity is just as sudden as the earlier one. With a violent jolt the Maiden is torn out of her sublime rapture. Her mission betrayed, she is immediately overcome with shame and guilt. She is disappointed in herself because she lacked the self-mastery, the moral stamina, to accomplish her object. Yet her fall contains the seeds of her renewal. After she has recovered her senses, her sole object is to regain what she lost.

Whereas in the first three acts we observe Joan in a state of moral sublimity steadfastly observing the requirements of her contract, in acts 4 and 5 her behavior becomes aesthetically sublime in the Schillerian sense. The third stage in the attainment of aesthetic sublimity is voluntary self-punishment to cancel wrongdoing. Expressed in the modern idiom, suffering is a moral detergent that gets out the toughest stain. The opportunity for atonement comes in the form of her father's denunciation for heresy and her subsequent banishment. By enduring the punishment for a crime of which she is innocent, she erases the one of which she is guilty. Her purification is symbolized in the drama by the cleansing storm. Emerging from it, she says that she has come to terms with herself and that she is now unaware of any other failings. Consequently, she possesses a new and higher kind of moral freedom because she chooses freely what she formerly only endured.

Joan gets a second chance to pit her will against her passion when Lionel confesses his love and begs her to marry him. This time she does not falter: "Nicht lieben kann ich dich" ("Love you, I never can," V, 9). When she renounces what her heart desires, she regains what she lost. Her old power returns. She breaks her chains asunder, rushes into battle, and turns defeat into victory not only for the French but also for herself because she is once again a chaste and pure spirit, not by God's doing but by her own.

The mind's ability to overcome what the appetites desire is a favorite topic with Schiller. In his drama the phenomenon appears as sublime behavior. In the characters of Karl Moor, Max Piccolomini, Mary Stuart, Joan of Arc, and Don Cesar moral duty clashes with inclination. In an epic struggle reason wins the day and the hero finds himself reborn into the realm of moral freedom. This theme also underlies Schiller's theory of social evolution. In his essay on aesthetic education, he links civilization's upward course directly to the development of the rational faculty. Again, in his essay *On the First Human Society*, he says that when man walked on all fours nature took care of him through instinct. Although unreasoning obedience to nature's voice guarantees survival, it is also a terrible bondage because at that stage man exists on the same level as the animals. He goes on to explain that mankind's ascent began when for the first time an unthinking creature felt the urge of instinct and chose not to act on it. This is the greatest event in history because it cut man off from nature's protective, but one-dimensional existence, introduced him to the world of alternatives, and set him on a course of unending progression. Modern man is superior to primitive man because he can choose how to form himself as individual and as species. Furthermore, Schiller thinks that the Eden myth, aside from its theological implications, may be a veiled retelling of man's first step out of nature. In eating the apple, Adam and Eve performed the first act of free will. They chose to disobey. In so doing, they lost the security of obedience but they gained the freedom to grow, change, mature, evolve. Now if we view *Die Jungfrau von Orleans* within this context, we see that it too retells the ascent of man and shows once again how Schiller's writings revolve around a few basic ideas.

In the beginning, Joan obeys blindly. She does not choose her mission but is chosen. As long as she acts unthinkingly, she enjoys protection from harm, error, guilt. She dwells in a state of sublime rapture. The Fall comes when she decides to spare Lionel. Disobedience expels her from divine protection: "Mit blinden Augen musstest du's vollbringen! /So bald du *sahst*, verliess dich Gottes Schild" ("With blind eyes you acted well! / But once you *saw*, God's shield abandoned you," IV, 1). As in Genesis, Joan is banished to the wilderness of freedom and to the agony of choice. She is on her own. But she uses her freedom to regain what she has lost. First, by accepting her punishment freely, she reduces it to a tool of expiation and thus celebrates a sublime victory over it. Next, in resisting the second temptation, and in asking God to restore her powers, she chooses a mission that was previously only endured.

Viewed within this context, Joan's mortal wound on the field of battle and her ecstatic last words symbolize her spiritual death and rebirth.

IV   Die Braut von Messina

The genesis of *Die Braut von Messina* [The Bride of Messina] begins as far back as 1776. In that year, the playwrights Leisewitz and Klinger both dramatized brotherly hatred and fratricide. Leisewitz's *Julius of Tarent* became young Schiller's favorite play. In that drama, the brothers Julius and Guido compete for the love of the same girl. The action climaxes at the end when Guido kills his brother in jealous rage and is himself killed by his outraged father. In Schiller's works, the theme of brotherly strife makes its first appearance in *Die Räuber* where villainous Franz destroys noble Karl. Schiller's plan to write another play on the same subject underwent many modifications until he finally started writing in August 1802. He completed the tragedy in February 1803, and it premiered on 9 March 1803 at the Weimar Hoftheater.

A   The Elements of the Plot

Although Schilller borrowed many motifs and techniques from classical Greek drama, the plot of *Die Braut von Messina* is his own creation. The long prehistory of the action on stage is revealed gradually as the story unfolds. Some twenty years earlier the widowed founder of Messina's ruling family had fallen in love with the young noblewoman Isabella and sought her hand in marriage. Isabella, however, chooses his son instead. During their wedding night the enraged king breaks into their apartment, rapes her, and as if this were not enough, curses her progeny forever: the fruit of her womb will be strife and hate. Eventually the king dies and his son ascends the throne. At about this time Isabella gives birth to twin sons. Don Manuel is an hour older than Don Cesar. Soon after their birth the king has a fearful dream. He sees two laurel trees spring up from his nuptial bed and intertwine their branches high above. Then a lily springs up between them, then turns into a flame which ignites the thick branches. Within moments the house is "consumed in monstrous tides of fire." Shaken, the king consults a Moor and interpreter of omens who pronounces that if Isabella has a daughter, the latter will cause the death of both sons and his dynasty will perish. Shortly thereafter Isabella has a dream of her own. She sees a little girl playing in the grass. A lion emerges from the forest with fresh prey. Then down from the sky swoops an eagle with a deer. Each places his kill beside the child and they settle down together peacefully. Puzzled, Isabella seeks out a Christian monk who tells her that she will bear a daughter who will unite her sons "in heisser Liebesglut" ("in the heat of ardent love").[7] Isabella understands "brotherly love." Shortly thereafter Isabella gives birth to Beatrice. To foil his fate, the king orders the infant flung into the sea. But Isabella disobeys. Aided only by her faithful servant Diego, she spirits the child away to a secluded convent, where she grows up in secrecy and in ignorance of her identity. No one ever discovers the truth.

About the time of Beatrice's birth the boys get into a childish dispute over an unspecified subject. Their anger persists and they grow to hate each other, thus fulfilling part of the ancient curse. But the evil does not end here. One day, while hunting in the forest, Don Manuel spies a deer, which he chases until it disappears through a convent gate. Inside, he finds the animal trembling at the feet of a beautiful maiden, Beatrice. It is love at first sight and soon Manuel is a nightly visitor. He tells no one of her existence. In addition, he neither tries to discover her identity nor does he reveal his own. Two months after their first encounter the king dies. Beatrice begs Manuel to take her to the funeral because, as she explains later, "Doch weiss ich nicht, welch bösen Sternes Macht / Mich trieb mit unbezwinglichem Gelüsten. / Des Herzens heissen Drang musst' ich vergnügen" ("And yet I do not know what evil star / Forced me with irresistible desire. / I had to satisfy my heart's strong impulse" III, 3). When he refuses, she charms Diego, and he agrees to take her there in disguise. At church she chances to sit beside her other brother, Don Cesar. Ignorant of their relationship they feel a strong attraction for each other. Driven by a "stille Schuld" ("Silent sin," II, 1), as she says, she soon slips away into the throng and forgets about her encounter. For Don Cesar, however, she becomes an obsession. He posts spies around town to watch for her.

Unaware of her effect on Don Cesar, she continues her relationship with Manuel. Then one day she learns from Diego that her unknown parents will take her away in a few days. When she relates the news to Manuel, he proposes marriage and they elope to Messina. There he hides her in a convent until the wedding. In the meantime he attends a meeting of reconciliation with his brother which Isabella has arranged. Left alone, Beatrice attends Vespers at the church across the street because, as she later relates, "mich trieb's mit mächt'gem Drang" ("a mighty urge drove me," II, 1).

Schiller takes up the action with the arrival of the brothers at the palace. Isabella pleads, argues, and implores her sons to reconcile their differences. Eventually, tentative remarks lead to the resolution of differences, and the meeting ends with a reconciliation. A messenger arrives who takes Cesar aside to tell him that one of his spies has found the girl he so desires. Cesar rushes to the church, where he announces without consultation that they will be wed within a few hours (II, 2). It is characteristic of his impetuous nature to leave without asking for her name.

When later in act 2 Isabella perceives that her sons are reconciled, she proudly reveals the existence of a sister who will arrive shortly. Overjoyed, Manuel and Cesar announce their own wedding plans. The scene ends with the family at the peak of happiness. They still do not know that the two brides, the sister, and the daughter are identical. Nobody realizes that Beatrice unites her brothers "in heisser Liebesglut" and so fulfills the prophecy.

In act 3 a series of reversals afflict the family. Faithful Diego enters with the news that pirates have kidnapped Isabella's daughter. During the ensuing conversation Manuel deduces from the incidents that he may be his sister's mate. His happiness fading rapidly, he hurries to the convent, where he confirms his suspicions. Before he can put things right, Cesar chances to walk in and sees them embracing. Convinced that his brother tricked him, he kills Manuel in a blind fury. Cesar returns to the palace unrepentant. When he learns from his mother that Beatrice is his sister and that he has killed Manuel in ignorance, remorse overwhelms him. Unable to live with his guilt, he decides to expiate his crime by taking his own life. Most of the fourth, and last act dramatizes the transforming effect of this decision upon his character.

B   The Drama as Classical Tragedy

Schiller was proud of *Die Braut von Messina*. In a letter he wrote to Humboldt on 17 February 1803 he tells him that "Mein erster Versuch einer Tragödie in strenger Form wird Ihnen Vergnügen machen. Sie werden daraus urteilen, ob ich, als Zeitgenosse des Sophokles, auch einmal einen Preis davon getragen haben möchte" ("My first attempt at a tragedy in the strictest form will please you. You can be the judge whether as Sophocles' contemporary I might have carried off a prize").[8] From this statement we conclude that one of the most productive ways of appreciating the play will be along the lines of Greek tragedy. Since the principles of tragedy were most clearly defined by Aristotle, and since Schiller had studied the *Poetics,* I will use Aristotle's list of criteria to structure the following analysis.

According to Aristotle's definition a tragedy "is an imitation of a noble and complete action, having the proper magnitude; it employs language that has been artistically enhanced by each of the kinds of linguistic adornment, applied separately in the various parts of the play; it is presented in dramatic, not narrative form, and achieves through the representation of pitiable and fearful incidents, the catharsis of such pitiable and fearful incidents."[9] Aristotle goes on to identify other criteria. The action should unfold in a proper order with a beginning, a middle, and an end. It should also be simple, and observe the unity of action. In order for us to feel pity and fear for the central character, he must be a man like, or better than, ourselves who passes from happiness to misery and who may or may not die. We are moved to pity only when his misfortune is greater than he deserves. He moves us to fear whenever we recognize part of ourselves in him or in his actions. Furthermore, the hero should commit some error, either out of ignorance or from a flaw in his character, *hamartia.* (The Greek tragedians favored pride.)

Plot is a central concept. Defined as the arrangement of the incidents, it is the means by which the author depicts the passage from happiness to suffering, evokes pity and fear, and induces catharsis; most important, it contains the two most powerful tragic emotions: *peripeteia* and *anagnorisis. Peripeteia* denotes the reversal from happiness to misery. It is often linked to *anagnorisis* which means the transition from ignorance to knowledge. Aristotle ranks a tragedy in which recognition coincides with reversal higher than one in which the two occur in different places. The most skillful use of recognition is when the hero deduces his knowledge from the incidents themselves rather than from indirect proof such as letters or word of mouth. Recognition of a close relative is the most effective.

Turning now to *Die Braut von Messina,* we see that it meets Aristotle's criteria. The action begins with the family in the joy of reunion and love. We admire the brothers for their ability to overcome their hatred and to end the deadly feud. Civil war has been averted and the family curse neutralized. After years of secluding her daughter, Isabella is thrilled about her imminent arrival. Likewise, her sons are both in love and each looks forward to his wedding. The family is at the peak of happiness and we are glad, for Isabella's account of the family's misfortune in her first monologue has evoked our pity. It seems their sufferings are more than they deserve. From here on the plot consists in nothing other than working out with mounting excitement and cunning delays how the curse fulfills itself. Soon we begin to suspect that Beatrice is not three different people but one and that the curse nears its culminating phase. That the cup of happiness runs over until the end of the third act does little to dispel our anxiety, for the fear that something may have happened is more intense than the knowledge that something has already happened or may happen in the future. Then when Manuel infers from the incidents themselves that he is his sister's mate, we experience a new kind of anxiety. Our discomfort is particularly acute when Manuel and Beatrice embrace, because we are afraid that Cesar might walk in. When Cesar slays his brother, the sensation of pity overtakes us once again. What has happened strikes us as unjust and avoidable. Now we experience fear as the tragic emotion proper when we recognize part of ourselves in this sequence of events. Though we may not be able to identify with the magnitude of their experiences, we often undergo the same ordeal on a smaller scale. Often we react impulsively under the stress of the unforeseen and later regret our hastiness. Likewise, we are sometimes misunderstood and suspected of acts of which we are innocent. The realization that something similar can befall us is frightening. Finally, the curtain falls on act 3 leaving us fearing for Isabella and Cesar who are still ignorant of the facts.

Cesar dispatches his brother's corpse to the palace. Its arrival turns Isabella's ecstatic reunion with her daughter into a nightmare of rage and sorrow. When Cesar comes and learns the whole truth, he too is plunged into misery. Cesar, however, gains knowledge from his mother's and sister's mouth rather than surmising it from the incidents, like Manuel. Since Aristotle says that the latter is the more skillful device, it seems that Schiller is technically at fault; that is, until we realize that it would be inconsistent with Cesar's mercurial temperament for him to derive the truth from the incidents, for that requires sober reflection. To convince, the method of discovery should fit the character. It speaks for Schiller's talent that he can make a technical fault work to advantage.

In the last act we experience the proper emotions once again. We fear that Isabella and Beatrice will be unable to dissuade Cesar from suicide. Yet at the same time we admire him in a new way, for he has undergone a rebirth in accordance with Schiller's theory of aesthetic sublimity. Serenity and calm have replaced hotheadedness. He accepts his guilt and expiates it, which evokes our admiration and gives us moral pleasure. At the same time we feel pity for him and all his family because their misfortune is more than they deserve.

Finally, we come away from the theater knowing something about the human condition and what causes tragedy.[10] We have learned, for instance, that deception, secrecy, and impulsiveness can lead us not only into misfortune but also into guilt which, as the chorus says, is the worst of all possible feelings:

> Dies *eine* fühl' ich und erkenn' es klar:
> Das Leben ist der Güter höchstes *nicht,*
> Der Übel grösstes aber ist die *Schuld.*

> One thing I clearly feel and here aver:
> Of all possessions life is not the highest,
> The worst of evils is, however, guilt.

(IV, 10)

The appeal of *Die Braut von Messina* lies primarily in its intellectualism and so reflects Schiller's ideas about the purpose of tragedy. In the essay *Über den Gebrauch des Chors in der Tragö-die* [On the Use of the Chorus in Tragedy], which is prefixed to the drama, Schiller says that tragedy should not be an emotional experience but an intellectual one in which we learn something about ourselves and life. When the spectator leaves the performance his psyche must not be the victim of impressions, "sondern sich immer klar und heiter von den Rührungen scheiden, die es [sein Gemüt] erleidet" ("but rather they must come away serene and clear from the agitations sustained"). Consequently, the artist must avoid the direct involvement of the spectator's emotions because one cannot reflect and have an emotional experience at the same time. This is Schiller's concept of aesthetic distance. It is not an attitude that the audience brings to the theater, but one which the tragedian builds into the play. There are many ways to do this. In our century Bertolt Brecht punctuated his productions with songs and encouraged the viewers to smoke in order to "alienate" them from the action on the stage. Schiller uses the chorus for a similar purpose.

Schiller claims that the chorus keeps the audience at arm's length by destroying the illusion of everyday reality. In the same essay we read: "So sollte er uns eine lebendige Mauer sein, die die Tragödie um sich herumzieht, um sich von der wirklichen Welt rein abzuschliessen" ("The chorus is a living wall that tragedy draws about itself in order to shut itself off from the real world"). In both Aristotle and Schiller the chorus is a character who participates in the action and who also steps outside the action to draw conclusions and to pronounce on universal principles. In so doing, "Der Chor *reinigt* also das tragische Gedicht, indem er die Reflexion von der Handlung absondert" ("The chorus *purifies* the tragic poem by dissociating reflection from the action"). The technique has the desired result in *Die Braut von Messina*. Whenever the action peaks, the chorus intervenes to keep us from getting involved. In the highly charged scene where Cesar goes from ignorance to knowledge, the chorus interrupts fifteen times.

This concludes the discussion of *Die Braut von Messina* as a tragedy in the Greek style. It now remains to examine the work as a *Schicksalsdrama* ("fate drama"), as it is sometimes called because it dramatizes the fulfillment of a curse and certain prophecies. What Schiller means by fate requires some clarification. The fatalist assumes the existence of incomprehensible and usually malevolent forces in the universe that foreordain the destiny of us all. We have no control over what happens to us. We are the playthings of gods. Activity, effort, and striving are futile because we cannot alter what Providence decrees. Our fate is like quicksand. The harder we struggle to get free the quicker we sink. Schiller's concept of fate is different, however. In his essays on poetry and on sublimity he admits that man is determined, not by supernatural forces but by his character. Man is subject, on the one hand, to impulses arising from his physical nature and to rational-cultural influences on the other. These forces shape a man's character. Character, in turn, determines how he reacts to chance and circumstance. Hence, a man's destiny grows out of his character. For Schiller fate, providence, destiny, and predestination are metaphors for biologically and sociologically determined behavior. As an idealist Schiller thinks that we can free ourselves from these forces.

In *Die Braut von Messina* chance and fate at first seem to be the ruling forces. It is apparently by chance that Manuel finds the convent where he meets his sister, it is by accident that Cesar sees Beatrice at the funeral; it is by chance again that she goes to Vespers where a spy sees her; it is by coincidence that Cesar misses a conversation that would have cleared up everything; and it is by chance that he returns to the convent garden and finds his brother holding Beatrice. This fantastic series of coincidences seems to mock the idea that man can control his destiny. Looking closer, however, we see that it is the result of the protagonists' impulsive character which creates the circumstances for chance to thrive. Beatrice attends the funeral because of a strong impulse; she attends Vespers for the same reason, Manuel abducts her impulsively, and virtually everything Cesar does is on impulse. Impulsiveness and passion are vehicles of the family curse. The chorus: "Es ist kein Zufall und blindes Los, / Dass die Brüder sich wütend selbst zerstören, / Denn verflucht ward der Mutter Schoss, / Sie sollte den Hass und den Streit gebären" ("It is no chance, no blind work of fate, / That these brothers destroy each other. / For to bear hatred and strife, / That was the curse on the womb of the mother").

The old king cursed Isabella because she preferred his son to him; hence, the tragedy is man-made. There is no oracle, no divine will at work, as there is in *Oedipus*. Sophocles wanted to show that man is subject to the will of the gods. Schiller, however, believes that man is responsible for his own life, that it is the flaws in human nature that make for tragedy. He believed with equal conviction that man can overcome his flaws, which explains why Don Cesar triumphs in the end. The curse did not specify that he must die, or that he must bear the responsibility for its fulfillment. Cesar chooses to take the responsibility, and he chooses to expiate the misery caused by the curse, which frees him and his family from it. At the end it is Cesar, not the curse, who controls events and dictates the future. Such is the message of the drama.

V   Wilhelm Tell

The genesis of *Wilhelm Tell* is unusual. It begins in 1797 when Goethe heard the legend while traveling in Switzerland. Back in Weimar he enthusiastically told Schiller about his plan to write an epic poem on the subject. But Goethe soon lost interest in the project. Then in early 1801 a persistent rumor had it that Schiller was secretly at work on a new drama called *Wilhelm Tell*. When word got back to Schiller in the form of serious inquiries, he denied it. Since he was just putting the final touches to *Die Jungfrau von Orleans*, he had not given the remotest thought to the subject. Then out of curiosity he decided to read the account of the Swiss hero in

Aigidius Tschudi's *Chronicon Helveticum* (1569?). A talented storyteller, Tschudi had collected all the legends about Tell, woven them into a single story, and claimed that he was reporting history. Tschudi's vivid account fired Schiller's imagination.

For the next two years Schiller collected books, maps, and pictures about Switzerland. He researched Swiss culture and geography to provide an aura of authenticity. In the final stages of composition it is said that his scriptorium resembled a Swiss tourist office. Work on the play began in August 1803. He finished it the following February. Schiller himself directed the first performance on 17 March 1804 at the Weimar Hoftheater. The drama was a great success and became immensely popular. Even the harshest critics liked it, singling out the use of local color for special praise.

Wilhelm Tell is a masterpiece of stagecraft. It represents in many ways the results of Schiller's long involvement with the Weimar Hoftheater. For several years he had directed performances there and listened to actors talk about drama from their standpoint. In addition, he had thoroughly studied the theatergoing public and got new insights into how best to evoke the proper reaction from the audience.

A   The Elements of the Plot

The curtain rises on a scene of rustic tranquillity on the banks of Lake Lucerne. A group of men stand at the ferry watching a storm approach from across the lake. The story begins when Baumgarten rushes up soaked in blood. He has just slain the tyrannical Vogt Wolfenschiessen with an ax for trying to force his wife. Imperial troopers are close behind him. He begs the ferryman Kuoni to take him across the lake to safety. Kuoni refuses because the storm-churned waves are too dangerous. At this moment Wilhelm Tell appears and, living up to his reputation as a master helmsman, ferries the fugitive across the stormy lake himself. The boat leaves shore just as the soldiers ride up. Enraged that their victim has escaped, they kill some nearby cattle to punish the men for helping Baumgarten to escape. In this fashion Schiller dramatizes in the first scenes the desperate situation that has developed in this part of Switzerland since the Austrain Emperor Ferdinand von Habsburg sent wicked governors with license to rule severely. The harshest of the harsh is the sadistic Vogt Hermann Gessler who, impelled by greed, exceeds the limits of his commission and tramples ancient rights underfoot. The forest cantons groan beneath his cruelty.

In the first three acts Schiller introduces the three separate plots which culminate in Swiss independence. The first, called the Rütli Confederacy, begins in act 1. Walter Fürst, Stauffacher, and Melchtal, who are citizens of different cantons, meet to discuss ways of alleviating the plight of their countrymen. They agree that assistance from the local aristocracy is out of the question. Baron von Attinghausen is well disposed but too advanced in years to lead a revolt. His nephew and heir, Ulrich von Rudenz, has become indifferent to his people. Now he plays courtier at Gessler's court in Altorf in hopes of winning the rich and beautiful Berta von Bruneck. Consequently, Fürst, Stauffacher, and Melchtal decide to take matters into their own hands. They agree that each of them will return to his home canton, where he will seek out ten trustworthy men and bring them to a secret clearing within the forest called the Rütli.

On the night of 7–8 November 1307 representatives from the three cantons meet upon the Rütli (II, 2). Following lengthy debate, they decide to use force to get their ancient rights restored, which they hope to accomplish without bloodshed. United in brotherhood, they transcend personal differences in the common cause. The revolt will be launched after Christmas.

The second plot, usually referred to as the Berta-Rudenz episode, is introduced in act 3. Rudenz declares his love to Berta and expresses his desire to marry her (III, 2). Although Berta is similarly inclined, she cannot approve of a man who has abandoned his people. Furthermore, she tells him that he commits a great folly in believing that the emperor will allow them to marry. Because Berta is heir to several large estates in Switzerland, the emperor has decided to marry her to a member of the Hapsburg family. Rudenz is therefore serving on the wrong side. If Switzerland is free, then so is she. Besides, she loves the Swiss. Soon alike in love and mind, they dedicate themselves to the cause of liberty.

The third and most famous story within the dramatic framework concerns the conflict between Wilhelm Tell and Vogt Gessler. Tell was absent from the meeting on the Rütli. Although sympathetic, he tells the confederates that he does not want to be involved in their deliberations. In his opinion the best course of action is one of nonprovocation. A peaceful man will be left at peace, he says. But Tell gets involved against his will. It happens when he takes his little boy Walter to Altorf in act 3. Tell has forgotten that Gessler has erected a pole with his hat on it in the town square and that everyone is ordered to genuflect before the hat to signify respect for the emperor. A severe punishment awaits anyone who refuses to obey. When Tell does not genuflect, imperial troopers seize him. Soon a large, threatening crowd gathers. Just as they are about to free Tell, Gessler rides up at the head of his retinue. There now ensues a famous scene.

Gessler hates Tell because when they once met alone on a narrow mountain pathway, he had involuntarily shown Tell his cowardly heart. Now he plans to take a special revenge. For snubbing the hat, Tell must shoot an apple from off his son's head at seventy paces. While Tell struggles with himself, Schiller distracts the audience's attention to a quarrel between Rudenz and Gessler. While everyone looks this way, Tell shoots his arrow and pierces the apple. Even Gessler praises the shot in amazement. But the famous archer's troubles have just begun. The Vogt asks him why he put a second arrow into his belt, promising not to kill him for a truthful answer. Tell replies that if the first arrow had struck his son, the second would now be in his lordship's heart. But the Vogt tricks him. He has promised only to spare Tell's life. So he orders him cast in chains and transported by ship to the dungeon at Küssnacht. That afternoon a terrific storm overtakes the vessel, giving Tell a chance to escape. Safe ashore, he realizes that he must kill Gessler to protect himself and his family from the retribution that is sure to follow. He decides to ambush the Vogt on the main road to Küssnacht at a narrow gorge called the Hohle Gasse. As the Vogt rides up, cursing the Swiss, Tell's arrow passes through his heart (IV, 3). So that the responsibility will not fall on the innocent, he emerges from his hiding place to reveal his identity.

The three independent plots are brought together in act 5. Although the armed revolt planned by the Rütli Confederacy was to occur after Christmas, they decide to act immediately in view of Gessler's death. They are joined by Rudenz. Most of the fifth act recounts the events of the successful revolt, which is accomplished without bloodshed. At this point Schiller introduces an episode which stands apart from the main line of the story. Duke Johannes of Swabia has recently murdered Emperor Ferdinand for cheating him of his inheritance. Now under the imperial ban, he wanders in these mountains disguised as a monk. He makes his way to Tell's cottage to ask for assistance. Tell becomes angry when Johannes likens his murder of Ferdinand to Tell's killing of Gessler. He at first refuses to help, but then relents when he perceives that

Johannes is remorseful. He gives him food before sending him on his way with advice as to how he might best expiate his crime.

The final scene opens out on the valley in front of Tell's cottage. His countrymen, the confederates, Berta and Rudenz, are all present. When Tell steps out on the front porch, they greet him with loud jubilation. All agree that Tell's bold deed was the spark that lit the fires of freedom.

B   *Wilhelm Tell as Monomyth*

This piece of art should not be judged according to the standards of high drama or measured against the principles of classical tragedy. *Wilhelm Tell* is a fairy tale, a folk legend, a myth transposed to the stage. Though the story is presented in dramatic form, its internal structure as a myth is still much in evidence. An effective way of approaching the play will be to seek the meaning in its structure. The following discussion surveys the chief components of the typical myth, then shows how Schiller makes use of them in the drama.

Joseph Campbell is among the best known writers on myth. After studying the myths of the ancient, Oriental, and Western world, Campbell shows that all of them follow a basic pattern. In *Hero With a Thousand Faces* he calls that common stucture the monomyth.[11] The typical hero of world mythology, he says, is a person of exceptional gifts. Often he enjoys special recognition for his talents. The world in which he lives suffers from some affliction, frequently symbolized by a dragon or an evil tyrant. The composite ogre figure also follows a common pattern. He is a blight on the countryside, a destroyer of the general welfare, a rapacious monster. The misery caused by him is described as being universal throughout the land. Cruel, malicious, and driven by egocentric urges, he destroys whatever he touches. Everywhere there is a longing cry for the liberating hero of the shining blade.[12]

The structure of the hero's adventure consists of three main stages, each of which has several subsections: (1) the separation or departure from the world of common day; (2) the road of trials and victories culminating in the acquisition of "the boon"; (3) the return. The first stage begins with signs of the hero's special talents and a call to use them for the general benefit. Sometimes the hero refuses the call. In such cases he is attacked and devoured by the being which stands guard at the entrance to the adventure realm; and the hero is forced upon his journey unwillingly. Once across the threshold the hero begins the main part of his adventure, where he undergoes a number of severe tests. In fairy tales and folk lore he battles awesome forces and beats them, often with magical aid. In the highly developed myths of advanced civilizations, the odyssey is into the hero's own psyche, the battles fought are with himself, and the victories won are moral. Finally, after a supreme ordeal, the hero attains the object of his quest, "the ultimate boon." The boon usually possesses magical powers. The power may be symbolized by a concrete object such as the Golden Fleece or, as in higher mythology, it may be the restoration of the flow of energy into the body of the world. Then, after more adventures which take place in the third stage, the hero returns to the world of common day where the boon restores the community to prosperity. Finally, his society honors him as redeemer.

The Tell episode follows closely the pattern of the monomyth. Appropriately, the story begins with a description of a land wasted by a ruthless tyrant. Like a green-eyed monster, Hermann Gessler lives in a beetling castle from which he makes frequent sorties to wreak havoc upon the countryside. Everywhere he is the same: minor infractions four-fold punished, sadistic cruelty, overweening malevolence, and widespread confiscation of property to sate his voracious appetite. Groaning beneath the weight of this evil lord, the community asks through the fisherman Ruodi: "Wann wird der Retter kommen diesem Lande?" ("When will a savior come into this land?" I, 1).[13]

The savior, of course, is Wilhelm Tell. His rescue of Baumgarten in the first scene demonstrates his special talents. We observe that his society looks up to him as a man of extraordinary gifts. The tales of his skill with the crossbow are legendary. He can hit a bird on the wing, clip an apple from the branch at a hundred paces. He is a master helmsman, an alpine hunter of uncommon skill, and a man of high moral principles. These great talents make him the country's natural leader. But as so often in the first stage, the hero refuses the call. He asks his comrades to exclude him from their activities. He keeps aloof because the mythological hero is never the chairman of a committee. Rather, he is a self-sufficient loner: "Der Starke ist am mächtigsten *allein*" ("A strong man is most mighty when *alone*," I, 3).

As in the monomyth, Tell embarks on his adventure unwillingly. He is forced into action by the guardian of the gate when the soldiers at the hatpole seize him for not genuflecting. The adventure begun, Tell undergoes three tests. He has to shoot an apple off his son's head, he has to escape from the tyrant, and he has to slay him. He accomplishes the first by virtue of his own talents. In the second, however, he requires supernatural aid, which comes in the form of the terrific storm which he artfully turns into the means of his escape. Awaiting Gessler in the Hohle Gasse, Tell does not debate the morality of his intentions. As in the myth, Schiller presents the forces of good and evil in terms of black and white. The villain is devoid of redeeming qualities and the hero is without blemish. Gessler is the voracious monster laying waste the countryside, and Tell is the hero prince come to slay him. And he does so with the same ease and sense of accomplishment as the Germanic hero Siegfried who kills the dragon Fafnir in *The Niflinga Saga*. After the shot, Tell appears symbolically on a cliff high above the crowd to take not the blame, but the recognition; not to justify, but to explain the nature and the function of the boon: "Frei sind die Hütten, sicher ist die Unschuld / Vor dir, du wirst dem Lande nicht mehr schaden." ("Our homes are free, the innocent are safe / From you. You will not further harm this land," IV, 3). In the final scene, the people gather to honor Tell as redeemer.

CHAPTER 5

Conclusion

S CHILLER ranks as Germany's foremost poet-philosopher and dramatist. Although he lived in the eighteenth century, it is unproductive to view him only within the context of a period, movement, or genre. He is in a special category of writers who outlive their time and who are as fresh today as when they wrote. Each generation discovers Schiller for itself and integrates him in some novel way. This phenomenon led one scholar to entitle his two-volume opus *Schiller, Contemporary of Every Epoch* (1976).[1] Schiller is also one of the few individuals whose ideas influence the course of civilization. Among other things, he affected philosophy (Hegel, Nietzsche), political theory (Marx), and psychology (Freud, Jung). There is an even smaller number of men who become part of the cultural environment. German towns that have no Schillerstrasse, Schillerplatz, or Gymnasium are few in number. The man in the street regards him as a national hero. In the nineteenth century his birthday was a holiday. All this leads me to the subject I wish to address in the conclusion. The question is neither where Schiller fits into literary history, politics, and aesthetics nor whom he influenced. Rather, which *ideas* are most influential and most relevant to us today in the United States? An effective way of approaching this task is to conduct a slightly playful interview between Schiller and the author of a book who is explaining him to the general reader.

AUTHOR: In *On the Aesthetic Education of Man* and in many of your other writings you indict our Western society for its degradation and its moral shallowness. You blast our single-minded preoccupation with getting and spending, our rapacious hedonism, our glorification of goal-oriented activity, our simulation, and particularly our inability to achieve anything other than technological progress. Can you explain what has gone wrong?

SCHILLER: Specialization, the fragmentation of society into sepa-

146

rate units carries most of the blame. This modern obsession with dividing and separating has become the structural principle of our civilization, it is even carried into the psyche itself, where feeling is sundered from reason, flesh from spirit. Psychic imbalance inhibits the individual's growth and consequently that of his civilization. The sad thing is that this deprivation is for nothing, because we can enjoy the benefits of technological *and* human progress.

AUTHOR: What do you mean by progress?

SCHILLER: We progress when we create circumstances that promote psychic unity.

AUTHOR: If we want to try out your system, where do we start?

SCHILLER: To simplify, we can begin by spending more time doing things just for the pleasure of it. We need to be more process-oriented. We must learn to play and to do so with a good conscience because play is the force that permeates the psyche and binds it together. And, above all, learn to play with beauty; for beauty as artistic semblance has the power to liberate us from the material world and all the determinations of our appetites.

AUTHOR: Are you saying that material things and sensual pleasure are wrong?

SCHILLER: No. Material things and sensual pleasure in themselves do not degrade, but the single-minded pursuit of them does. A life oriented around indulging the appetites is transitory, temporary, and ultimately unsatisfying. If we live according to the principle that happiness lies in the reward we receive for getting things done, rather than in the activity itself, we project happiness outside of ourselves where it becomes an object that we pursue instead of a condition that we create for ourselves. To get the most out of existence "Fliehet aus dem engen, dumpfen Leben / In des Ideales Reich" ("Leave life's stupefying narrowness / For the realm of ideals").[3]

AUTHOR: How do we go from here to there?

SCHILLER: By prying ourselves loose from the material world. The tool for that is semblance, artistic illusion, *Schein*.

AUTHOR: I still do not understand how semblance frees.

SCHILLER: Semblance is form separated from matter. It exists only in the eye like a rainbow, or a shadow, or a painting. Semblance cannot be touched, eaten, or traded in on a new model. Now since we can possess only what has matter, if there is no matter, then there is nothing to possess. If there is nothing to possess, then there is nothing to desire. If there is nothing to desire, the appetites are neutralized, and the psyche dwells in the realm of aesthetic semblance.

AUTHOR: You mean to say all this happens without my knowledge?

SCHILLER: Yes. I have analyzed the mechanics of the process making it available to the conscious mind. Now I propose that we use art systematically as an educational device for ultimately making the aesthetic condition man's permanent state of mind, rather than the fleeting experience that it is now.

AUTHOR: Your theory preaches the self-deification of man!

SCHILLER: It does, if by that we mean the development of potential. The full realization of potential is what we attribute to the gods. But instead of recognizing divine qualities as merely our own inner ideal projected outward and upward, we regard it as unattainable, or we transport it to a Hereafter (XV, 9).[3] Ideal man, by contrast, perceives the image within himself and makes its approximation his life's task. He comes to regard himself and what he does as its own value. Like the gods, he is self-sufficient, self-contained, a law unto himself.

AUTHOR: If everyone is his own law, what restrains him in his relationship to others?

SCHILLER: The basic principle of the aesthetic realm is that our actions have no secondary motive. Consequently, ideal man treats others as he plays and as he treats himself; that is, as an end in themselves.

AUTHOR: Are you saying that your ideal man is free from the routine, the annoyances, and the vicissitudes of daily life?

SCHILLER: Not at all. The difference lies in the way he transcends them by doing more than necessary. When a man does what he has to do with superfluous grace, he transports himself and his activity into the higher sphere of aesthetic appearance. He is still part of this world but he is above it at the same time, like the gods.

AUTHOR: Can you give me an example?

SCHILLER: Consider Greek sculpture. As I explain in the *Fifteenth Letter*, the thing we notice about their representation of deities is what the marble does *not* express: The faces are smooth, unfurrowed by labor, worry, emotional pain, or material want. They betray no conflict either within themselves or without. They are free from the marks of experience. They are above it all. The figures as a whole express not just innocence, but a kind of innocence resulting from the harmonious fusion of innocence and knowledge. Likewise for the man who cultivates the aesthetic attitude. He transcends his earthly limitations. He inhabits a realm of pure appearance quite apart from the real world, but not alienated from it. There, the reconciliation of all polarity is possible; there, both sides of our psyche are engaged equally.

AUTHOR: Is it not dangerous to confuse illusion and reality?

SCHILLER: There is no danger. The illusion which I mean is not simulation; rather, it is aesthetic semblance, pure appearance. We recognize it and enjoy it for what it is.

AUTHOR: Well, what does the aesthetic attitude feel like?

SCHILLER: You mean the physical and mental sensation of being in a state of utter repose and supreme agitation simultaneously? "Jene wunderbare Rührung, für welche der Verstand keinen Begriff und die Sprache keinen Namen hat" ("There results that wondrous stirring for which mind has no concept nor speech any name," XV, 9). Examine the pleasurable experience you have when listening to good music, or when viewing your favorite work of art. That pleasure is the sensation of harmony; that is how the aesthetic condition feels.

AUTHOR: Why, your whole theory is rooted in *this* world and emphasizes the pleasure principle.

SCHILLER: Do you prefer suffering, humility, and renunciation? Whatever we pass up here is not going to be waiting for us in eternity. We must learn to appreciate the fact that man is a playful and creative animal with a faculty for pleasure. By pleasure I do not only mean things like the trysting hour's thousand delights or the frozen rhapsodies of elegant thought. I mean that nameless sensation that arises when both synthesize into one. It happens on one level when we play a game, it happens on a higher one when we ornament our speech and deeds with grace, and it happens on the highest where we create art and ideas.

AUTHOR: "The trysting hour's?" No one speaks in such a manner. Why not simply erotic pleasure?

SCHILLER: That is what I mean by embellishing our activities with superfluous grace. Something to delight the ear while informing the mind. People would speak more gracefully if they could enjoy the benefits of aesthetic education.

AUTHOR: I am having difficulty envisioning a government operating on aesthetic principles, even your particular kind.

SCHILLER: That is because there is no government as political organization. Since the citizen becomes the ideal, he is himself the state. Political organization is a relic of unbalanced antiquity. In its place is culture as the shaping force, public opinion the only pressure needed (XXVI, 12).

AUTHOR: Awhile ago we were speaking of civilization. How does that differ from culture?

SCHILLER: Superfluity versus utility, multiplicity versus standardization, a Greek vase versus a styrofoam cup.

AUTHOR: What, then, is the role of culture?

SCHILLER: Ideally, culture cultivates the aesthetic attitude in the individual citizen and in society at large. It watches over the boundaries between the drives while developing both. By providing the sense-drive with multiplicity of experience, the surface area expands thereby enabling it to apprehend more of the world. At the same time, culture stimulates the rational faculty, deepening and broadening the understanding. Most important of all, it concentrates on refining the capacity for appreciating beauty, or what we call taste. It teaches the individual to play with his eyes and his ears, it shows him how to separate semblance from substance and to enjoy it as its own value. It teaches him not to enjoy more, but differently. It gives him the best of both worlds.

AUTHOR: It sounds like an interesting utopian scheme.

SCHILLER: It is not utopian. Utopian systems want to replace existing ones. I am adding to what we already have. My theory emphasizes the free development and the right use of faculties we already possess. The aesthetic state as political organization and the aesthetic condition as an individual attitude of mind are not either/or totalities. We possess them in degree, like truth and freedom. So unlike in the case of utopian schemes, we need not wait until some far off future perfect. We can enjoy it now. As a potential, everyone has it. As a present reality, we see good approximations in certain individuals and in small groups. As a future possibility the whole of society could transform itself. But that would take over a hundred years, even if we started right now by introducing aesthetic education into the school curriculum.

AUTHOR: How do you recommend that we organize our school curriculum?

SCHILLER: How should I know? I am a man of ideas, not a tactician. I observe nature, I study animal and human behavior, I read history and philosophy, I contemplate art, I introspect (I, 2). From this I derive a theory. Then come the technicians. Their job is to translate ideas into reality.

AUTHOR: Your detractors castigate your system because it disallows the oppressed classes to redress grievances through revolution. They say you support the status quo.

SCHILLER: That depends. As I aver in *Wilhelm Tell*, the use of force produces good results under two conditions. The citizen must not have any other alternative, and he must be prepared for the freedom he seeks. Under any other circumstances brute force is undesirable because it easily turns its users into brutes. So employ it only as a last resort, and exert it with calm determination. Avoid passion because that leads to unnecessary bloodshed. A revolution ignoring these facts will harm the society it seeks to benefit. Look at the French Revolution where force has degenerated into revengeful butchery. Is the Committee for Public Safety in Paris creating circumstances favorable to psychic unity? Is French civilization taking a step forward? The opposite is true. With bands playing and flags waving, France marches backward into barbarism. In this particular case the status quo *is* better.

AUTHOR: Yes, but is your theory workable? Your adversaries say that it looks good on paper but that it is probably unattainable and impractical besides.

SCHILLER: You are forgetting that my theory merely systematizes what already exists. So how can it be said that my theory is unworkable when you can see it in action all around you? In a larger sense, the objections are beside the point, for ideas such as these transcend the importance of attainability and practicality. Just by thinking on so grand a scale, humanity not only enlarges its universe but expands and ennobles itself.

AUTHOR: Well, what advice do you have for someone who would like to try out your theory on a personal level right now?

SCHILLER: "An dem Scheine mag der Blick sich weiden" ("Feast your eyes on semblance").[4]

Notes and References

Chapter One

1. All citations are to *Schillers Sämtliche Werke*, Säkular-Ausgabe, ed. E. von der Hellen et al., 16 vols. (Stuttgart, 1904–1905). Hereafter, *Werke*.

2. *Werke*, 12:8. Translations are to *On the Aesthetic Education of Man*, ed. and trans. Elizabeth M. Wilkinson and L. A. Willoughby (Oxford, 1967). Future references appear in the text by letter (roman numeral) and paragraph (arabic numeral).

3. Friedrich Nietzsche, *Werke in Drei Bänden*, ed. Karl Schlechta (Munich: Hanser, 1955), 2:1004; my translation.

4. Fyodor Dostoevsky, *The Brothers Karamazov*, trans. Constance Garnett (New York: Random House, 1950), p. 734.

5. *Werke*, 12:169. The translation is to *Naive and Sentimental Poetry. On the Sublime*, trans. Julius A. Elias (New York, 1966).

6. Fyodor Dostoevsky, *Crime and Punishment*, trans. Constance Garnett (New York: Random House, 1950), p. 406.

7. *Ibid.*, p. 269.

8. *Ibid.*, p. 530.

Chapter Two

1. *Werke*, vol. 1.

2. Nenie was the goddess of funerals. Songs sung at funerals were called "nenie." *Stygischen Zeus:* Hades. *Einmal nur:* the reference is to Orpheus and Eurydice. *Schattenbeherrscher:* Hades. *Aphrodite:* As a favor to jealous Persephone, Ares transformed himself into a boar and fatally gored Aphrodite's lover Adonis before her eyes. *Skäischen Tor:* a gate of Troy. The reference is to Achilles and his mother Thetis, a sea-divinity. The daughters of Nereus are her sisters.

Chapter Three

1. *Werke*, vol. 3; my translations.

2. *Ibid;* my translations.

3. *Ibid.*, 12:263.

4. *Ibid.*, vol. 4. The reference is to *Don Carlos*, trans. Charles E. Passage (New York, 1959).

5. *Werke*, 16:65.

Chapter Four

1. *Werke*, vol. 5. The reference is to *Wallenstein*, trans. Charles E. Passage (New York, 1959).

2. *Briefe*, ed. Fritz Jonas, Kritische Gesamtausgabe, 7 vols. (Stuttgart, 1892–1896), 5:21.

3. *Ibid.*, 5:478–79.

4. *Werke*, vol. 6. The reference is to *Mary Stuart*, trans. Charles E. Passage (New York, 1961).

5. *Werke*, 12:263.

6. *Werke*, vol. 6. The reference is to *The Maid of Orleans*, trans. Charles E. Passage (New York, 1961).

7. *Werke*, vol. 7. The reference is to *The Bride of Messina*, trans. Charles E. Passage (New York, 1961).

8. *Briefe*, 7:13.

9. Aristotle, *Poetics*, trans. Leon Golden (Englewood Cliffs: Prentice Hall, 1968), p. 11.

10. For a more elaborate discussion of catharsis see: Leon Golden, "Mimesis and Katharsis," *Classical Philology* 64 (1969): 145–53.

11. Joseph Campbell, *Hero With a Thousand Faces* (Princeton: Princeton University Press, 1949), pp. 35–40.

12. I am paraphrasing Campbell.

13. *Werke*, vol. 7. The reference is to *Wilhelm Tell*, trans. Charles E. Passage (New York, 1962).

Chapter Five

1. Robert Oellers, *Schiller: Zeitgenosse aller Epochen*, 2 vols. (Munich, 1976).

2. From the poem *Das Ideal und das Leben* [The Ideal and Life].

3. The roman numeral refers to the number of the letter, the arabic numeral refers to the paragraph.

4. *Das Ideal und das Leben*.

Selected Bibliography

BIBLIOGRAPHICAL SOURCES

1. German bibliographies

Schiller, Bibliographie 1893–1958. Edited by Wolfgang Vulpius. Weimar: Aufbau-Verlag, 1959.

Schiller, Bibliographie 1959–1963. Edited by Wolfgang Vulpius. Berlin: Aufbau-Verlag, 1967.

Schiller, Bibliographie 1959–1961. Edited by P. Raabe and Ingrid Bode. *Jahrbuch der deutschen Schillergesellschaft* 10 (1962): 465–553.

Schiller, Bibliographie 1962–1965. Edited by Ingrid Bode. *Jahrbuch der deutschen Schillergesellschaft* 10 (1966): 465–505.

Schiller, Bibliographie 1966–1969 und Nachträge. Edited by Ingrid Bode. *Jahrbuch der deutschen Schillergesellschaft* 14 (1970): 584–636.

2. English bibliographies

American Schiller Literature: A Bibliography. Edited by John R. Frey. In *Schiller 1759–1959: Commemorative American Studies.* Urbana: University of Illinois Press, 1959. Pp. 203–13.

Schiller in England 1787–1960: A Bibliography. Edited by Richard Pick. *Publications of the English Goethe Society* 30 (1961): 832–62.

PRIMARY SOURCES

1. German editions

Schillers Sämmtliche Schriften. Historisch-kritische Ausgabe. Edited by Karl Goedeke. Stuttgart: Cotta, 1867–1869.

Schillers Sämtliche Werke: Säkular-Ausgabe. Edited by E. von der Hellen. Stuttgart: Cotta, 1904–1905.

Schillers Werke: Nationalausgabe. Edited by Julius Petersen. Weimar: Böhlau, 1943–. This edition is not yet complete.

Friedrich Schiller: Sämtliche Werke. Edited by Gerhard Fricke. Munich: Hanser, 1958–1959.

2. English translations

The Works of Frederick Schiller. Translated by A. J. W. Morrison. 4 vols. London: 1846–1849.

Complete Works. Translated by S.T. Coleridge, Baron Lytton, and others.

155

Edited, with careful revisions and new translations by C. J. Hempel. 2
vols. Philadelphia: Bohn, 1870.

Friedrich Schiller: An Anthology for our Time. In new English translations
and the original German. With an account of his life and work by
Frederick Ungar. New York: Ungar, 1959. A general introduction
containing selections from the prose, poetry, and drama.

The Bride of Messina, Wilhelm Tell, Demetrius. Translated by Charles E.
Passage. New York: Ungar, 1962. With an introduction.

Don Carlos. Translated by Charles E. Passage. New York: Ungar, 1959.
With an introduction.

Naive and Sentimental Poetry, On the Sublime. Translated by Julius Elias.
New York: Ungar, 1966. With an introduction and notes.

Mary Stuart, The Maid of Orleans. Translated by Charles E. Passage. New
York: Ungar, 1961. With an introduction.

On the Aesthetic Education of Man in a Series of Letters. Translated by
Reginald Snell. New York: Frederick Ungar, 1965. With an introduction.

On the Aesthetic Education of Man in a Series of Letters. Edited and
translated by E. M. Wilkinson and L. A. Willoughby. Oxford: Clarendon Press, 1967. Dual language edition with an introduction, commentary, and glossary of terms.

Wallenstein. Translated by Charles E. Passage. New York: Ungar, 1959.
With an introduction.

SECONDARY SOURCES

BERGER, KARL. *Schiller. Sein Leben und seine Werke.* Munich: Beck, 1905.
Life and works. Representative of the nineteenth century view.

BERGHAHN, KLAUS. "Ästhetik und Politik im Werk Schillers: Zur jüngsten
Forschung." *Monatshefte* 66 (1974): 401–21. Reviews nine books
published between 1967 and 1973. Discusses trends in Schiller schol-
arship.

BINDER, WOLFGANG. "Die Begriffe 'naive' und 'sentimentalisch' und Schillers Drama." *Jahrbuch der deutschen Schillergesellschaft* 4 (1960): 140–
57.

BRUFORD, W.E. *Culture and Society in Classical Weimar.* Cambridge:
Cambridge University Press, 1962. Provides a picture of Schiller's
times.

BUCHWALD, REINHARD. *Schiller: Leben und Werk.* 2 vols. Leipzig: Insel,
1937. Biography coupled with an analysis of the meaning of his major
works. Fluent style.

BURSCHELL, FRIEDRICH. *Schiller.* Hamburg: Rowohlt, 1968. Aims at giving
a true-to-life picture of Schiller free of distortions.

BUTTLER, ELIZABETH MARION. *The Tyranny of Greece over Germany.*
Cambridge: Cambridge University Press, 1935. Explores the influence
of the Greeks on several great German writers, including Schiller.

CARLYLE, THOMAS. *The Life of Friedrich Schiller.* London: Chapman and Hall, 1825. Still readable and informative.

DAEMMRICH, HORST. "Friedrich Schiller and Thomas ˘Mann: Parallels in Aesthetics." *Journal of Aesthetics and Art Criticism* 19 (1965–1966): 227–49.

DEWHURST, KENNETH, AND REEVES, NIGEL. *Friedrich Schiller: Medicine, Psychology, and Literature.* Berkeley: University of California Press, 1978. Translations and commentary. The first English edition of his complete medical and psychological writings. How his knowledge of medicine influenced his philosophical and aesthetic theories.

DUSING, WOLFGANG. "Kosmos und Natur in Schillers Lyrik." *Jahrbuch der deutschen Schillergesellschaft* 13 (1969): 196–220.

EBSTEIN, FRANCES. "In Defense of Marquis Posa." *Germanic Review* 36 (1961): 204–20.

ENGEL, EVA. "Schiller on the Nature of Evil." *Publications of the English Goethe Society* 37 (1967): 31–56.

EVANS, BLAKEMORE. "*Die Jungfrau von Orleans:* A Drama of Philosophical Idealism." *Monatshefte* 35 (1943): 188–94.

FOWLER, FRANK. "Schiller's Fiesko Reexamined." *Publications of the English Goethe Society* 40 (1970): 1–29.

GARLAND, HENRY B. *Schiller.* London: Harrap, 1949. A general introduction.

GOLDEN, LEON. "Mimesis and Katharsis." *Classical Philology* 54 (1969): 145–53.

GILLESPIE, GERALD. "Freedom of Conscience in Schiller and Lohenstein." *Kentucky Foreign Language Journal* 13 (1966): 237–46.

GRAHAM, ILSE. *Schiller's Drama: Talent and Integrity.* New York: Barnes and Noble, 1974. Concentrates on the "thematic, artistic, and aesthetic idiosyncrasies which constitute the poet's signature."

GRONICKA, ANDRE VON. "Friedrich Schiller's Marquis Posa: A Character Study." *Germanic Review* 26 (1951): 196–214.

GROSSMANN, WALTER. "Schiller's Philosophy of History in His Jena Lectures of 1789–90." *Publications of the Modern Language Association* 69 (1954): 156–72.

————. "The Idea of Cultural Evolution in Schiller's Aesthetic Education." *Germanic Review* 34 (1959): 39–49.

GUTHKE, KARL S. "Räuber Moors Glück und Ende." *German Quarterly* 39 (1966): 1–11.

HAMBURGER, KÄTE. "Schiller und Sartre. Ein Versuch zum Idealismus Problem Schillers." *Jahrbuch der deutschen Schillergesellschaft* 3 (1959): 34–70.

HAUPT, JOHANNES. "Geschichtsperspektive und Griechenverständnis im ästhetischen Programm Schillers." *Jahrbuch der deutschen Schillergesellschaft* 18 (1974): 407–30.

HEITNER, ROBERT R. "Luise Millerin and the Shock Motif in Schiller's Early Dramas." *Germanic Review* 41 (1966): 27–44.

HERMAND, JOST. "Schillers Abhandlung 'Über Naive und Sentimentalische Dichtung' im Lichte der deutschen Popularphilosophie des 18. Jahrhunderts." *Publications of the Modern Language Association* 79 (1964): 428–41.

HINDERER, WALTER, ed. *Schillers Dramen: Neue Interpretationen.* Stuttgart: Reclam, 1979. Twelve essays.

JAMESON, FREDERIC. *Marxism and Form.* Princeton: Princeton University Press, 1971. With a chapter on Schiller.

JOHNSTON, OTTO. "Schiller, Diderot and the Dalberg Manuscript." *Germanic Review* 46 (1971): 167–81.

KAUFMANN, W. F. *Schiller: Poet of Philosophical Idealism.* Oberlin: Academy Press, 1942.

KERRY, S. S. *Schiller's Writings on Aesthetics.* Manchester: Manchester University Press, 1961. How "linguistic functions . . . lead progressively to a concentrated pattern of ideas."

KOOPMANN, HELMUT. *Friedrich Schiller.* 2 vols. Stuttgart: Metzler, 1966. Introduction to life, works, and criticism.

––––––. *Schiller-Kommentar.* Munich: Winkler Verlag, 1969.

KORFF, HERMANN A. *Geist der Goethezeit.* Leipzig: Koehler und Amelang, 1923. Schiller within the eighteenth century.

KÜHNEMANN, EUGEN. *Schiller.* Munich: Beck, 1905. Life and works.

LANGER, SUSAN. *Feeling and Form.* New York: Charles Scribner's Sons, 1953. A theory of art with Schiller's *Schein* as the major building block.

LUKÁCS, GEORG. *Goethe und seine Zeit.* Berlin: Aufbau Verlag, 1955.

MAINLAND, WILLIAM P. *Schiller and the Changing Past.* London: Heinemann, 1957. A general introduction.

MARLEYN, R. "Wallenstein and the Structure of Schiller's Tragedies." *Germanic Review* 32 (1957): 186–99.

MICHELSEN, PETER. "Studien zu Schillers Räubern. *Jahrbuch der deutschen Schillergesellschaft* 8 (1964): 57–111.

MILLER, R. D. *The Drama of Schiller.* Harrogate: Duchy Press, 1963. Textual criticism.

––––––. *Schiller and the Ideal of Freedom.* Oxford: Clarendon Press, 1970. An exposition of the philosophical works with chapters on Kant.

MÜLLER-SEIDEL, WALTER. "Das stumme Drama der Luise Millerin." *Goethe* 17 (1955): 91–103.

NERJES, GÜNTER. "Schiller and Karl August von Weimar." *Monatshefte* 56 (1964): 273–80.

NORMAN, F., ED. Schiller. *Bicentenary Lectures.* London: University of London Institute of Germanic Languages and Literatures, 1960. Essays by Purdie, Stahl, Wilkinson, von Wiese, Graham, Witte.

OELLERS, NORBERT. *Schiller: Zeitgenosse aller Epochen.* 2 vols. Munich: Beck, 1976. Documents the attitude to Schiller of well-known figures from 1782 to 1966.

PASSAGE, CHARLES E. *Friedrich Schiller.* New York: Ungar, 1975. Introduction to life and works.

PRADER, FLORIAN. *Schiller und Sophokles.* Zürich: Atlantis, 1954.

PRAWER, SIEGBERT S. "What did Karl Marx Think of Schiller?" *German Life and Letters* 29 (1975): 122–37.

REGIN, DEREK. *Freedom and Dignity.* The Hague: Nijhoff, 1965. "It is basically devoted to his ideas on freedom."

RYDER, FRANK. "Schiller's *Tell* and the Cause of Freedom." *German Quarterly* 48 (1975): 487–504.

SAMMONS, JEFFREY. "Mortimer's Conversion and Schiller's Allegiances." *Journal of English and Germanic Philology* 72 (1973): 155–66.

SEIDLIN, OSKAR. "Schiller: Poet of Politics." In *A Schiller Symposium,* edited by Leslie Willson. Austin: University of Texas Press, 1960.

SELLNER, TIMOTHY F. "The Lionel Scene in Schiller's *Jungfrau von Orleans:* A Psychological Interpretation." *German Quarterly* 50 (1977): 264–82.

SILZ, WALTER. "Antithesis in Schiller's Poetry." *Germanic Review* 34 (1959): 165–84.

SIMONS, JOHN D. "The Nature of Oppression in Don Carlos." *Modern Language Notes* 84 (1969): 451–57.

———. "The Myth of Progress in Schiller and Dostoevsky." *Comparative Literature* 24 (1972): 328–37.

STAHL, E. L. *Friedrich Schiller's Drama: Theory and Practice.* Oxford: Clarendon Press, 1954. His drama examined in the light of his philosophical theories.

STAIGER, EMIL. *Friedrich Schiller.* Zürich: Atlantis-Verlag, 1967. A standard work. Presupposes familiarity with Schiller's life and work.

STORZ, GERHARD. *Der Dichter Friedrich Schiller.* Stuttgart: Klett, 1963. Focuses mainly on the dramas. Aimed at specialists.

THALHEIM, HANS-GÜNTER. "Schillers Dramen von *Maria Stuart* bis *Demetrius.* Teil I." *Weimarer Beiträge* 20 (1974): 5–33.

THOMAS, CALVIN. *The Life and Works of Friedrich Schiller.* New York: Henry Holt, 1901. A general introduction.

WATERMAN, JOHN T. "*Die Jungfrau von Orleans* in the light of Schiller's Essays." *German Quarterly* 25 (1952): 230–38.

WEIGAND, HERMANN J. *Surveys and Soundings in European Literature.* Edited by Leslie Willson. Princeton: Princeton University Press, 1966. With three essays on Schiller.

WELLS, G. A. "Schiller's View of Nature in *Über Naive und Sentimentalische Dichtung.*" *Journal of English and Germanic Philology* 65 (1966): 491–510.

———. "Fate Tragedy and Schiller's *Die Braut von Messina.*" *Journal of English and Germanic Philology* 64 (1965): 191–212.

WIESE, BENNO VON. *Friedrich Schiller,* 4th ed. Stuttgart: Metzler, 1978. A standard volume on life and works.

WILKINSON, ELIZABETH M. "Schiller's Concept of *Schein* in the Light of Recent Aesthetics." *German Quarterly* 28 (1955): 219–27.

WILLOUGHBY, L. A. "Schiller on Man's Education to Freedom through Knowledge." *Germanic Review* 29 (1954): 163–74.

WITTE, WILLIAM. *Schiller*. Oxford: Blackwell's, 1949. A general introduction.

WITTKOWSKI, WOLFGANG. "Friedrich Schiller 1962–1965: Ein Literaturbericht." *Jahrbuch der deutschen Schillergesellschaft* 10 (1966): 414–64.

ZELLER, BERNHARD, ED. *Schiller: Reden im Gedenkjahr 1959*. Stuttgart; Klett, 1961. Twenty-three essays.

ZIOLKOWSKI, THEODORE. *The Classical German Elegy*. Princeton: Princeton University Press, 1980. Discovers an unknown genre begun by *Der Spaziergang*.

Index